# THE
# THINNING
# BLUE LINE

## ADDRESSING THE LAW ENFORCEMENT
## VACANCY CRISIS

### COLIN WHITTINGTON

To request permission, contact Colin Whittington
colin.whittington@recruitingheroesllc.com
571-242-2899


ISBN: 979-8-218-62852-9
Library of Congress Control Number:

Printed in the United States of America

First Edition: February 2025


Published by Recruiting Heroes LLC
Boyce, Virginia
WhittingtonBooks.com

# DEDICATION

This book is dedicated to the women and men serving on the Thin Blue Line who bravely step into the line of fire, safeguarding our way of life with courage and dedication.

# ALSO BY COLIN WHITTINGTON

## Beyond the Thin Blue Line

Beyond the Thin Blue Line is a comprehensive career guide for Police Officers, Deputy Sheriffs, Correctional Officers, and Federal Agents considering leaving law enforcement. It provides step-by-step guidance on writing a professional resume, optimizing LinkedIn profiles, leveraging networking opportunities, salary negotiations, job search strategies, and much more. The book includes inspirational stories from former officers who have successfully transitioned to new careers, offering practical tips and diverse perspectives. Finally, the six-month roadmap gives you specific steps to complete as you come to the end of your law enforcement career.

*"This is a must-read for anyone thinking about moving on from law enforcement or the military to the private sector."*
**-- Sheriff Mike Chapman**

Sheriff – Loudoun County Sheriff's Office, 2023 "National Sheriff of the Year", Vice President – Homeland Security Committee

Visit WhittingtonBooks.com to get your copy of Beyond the Thin Blue Line

# CONTENTS

# CHAPTER ONE
# THE PERFECT STORM

Imagine a world where the streets are deserted, not from the comfort of safety but from the grip of fear. The once happily bustling neighborhoods, now shadowed by an eerie silence, have become battlegrounds for the ruthless, the greedy, and the desperate. Without law enforcement, the Thin Blue Line that separates order from chaos would vanish, leaving communities vulnerable to the whims of those who thrive in the absence of authority. Businesses would shut their doors at dusk, not from the chill of nightfall but from the terror of what lurks in the dark. Emergency calls would go unanswered, leaving society's most vulnerable without the resources to survive another day. The very fabric of society would begin to unravel as trust is replaced by survival instincts, and every individual—man, woman, or child—is left to fend for themselves in a world teetering on the brink of anarchy. This is not dystopian fiction. This is the horrifying reality that could emerge if the crippling law enforcement vacancy crisis is not addressed.

Law enforcement in America has a rich and complex history, tracing its origins back to the early colonial era when communities relied on informal, often volunteer, watchmen and constables to maintain order. As the nation grew and urbanized, the need for more organized and professional police forces became evident, leading to the establishment of the first formal police departments in the mid-19th century. These early developments marked a significant shift from community-driven policing to a more structured approach, reflecting the increasing demands of a rapidly industrializing society. Over the decades, law enforcement evolved to address new challenges, such as rising crime rates, labor unrest, and the impacts of mass immigration, all while grappling with issues of corruption, excessive force, and the policing of marginalized communities.

Understanding this historical context highlights law enforcement's pivotal role in maintaining societal stability across different eras of American history. Today, as the law enforcement profession faces unprecedented challenges, including public scrutiny, calls for reform, and the impact of modern technology, the stakes are higher than ever. Due to these diverse obstacles, law enforcement is experiencing a historic staffing crisis. This is not just a momentary disruption but a potential turning point that could reshape the future of policing in America. By looking back at how law enforcement has adapted and transformed over time, we can gain deeper insights into the significance of this moment and the profound implications it holds for the future of public safety and social order.

Across the nation, law enforcement agencies are experiencing a sharp decline in police officers, deputy sheriffs, correctional officers, and other law enforcement professionals. This shortage is so severe in some areas that the grim scenario of lawlessness is becoming a daily reality for millions of Americans. Local, state, and federal law enforcement, crippled by a lack of resources, are struggling to properly serve and protect their communities. Vacancy rates in many departments now range from 10% to 30% or more, leaving hundreds or thousands of positions unfilled nationwide. A 2019 study by the International Association of Chiefs of Police (IACP) found that 78% of the country's roughly 18,000 law enforcement agencies had difficulties recruiting qualified candidates, with 75% feeling that recruiting challenges had worsened in the last five years. Shockingly, 50% of these agencies reported altering their policies and procedures due to low staffing levels, often resulting in diminishing services for their communities.

COLIN WHITTINGTON

Since the IACP study was published, the law enforcement vacancy crisis has deepened significantly, fueled by generational changes and transformative societal events that have reshaped public perceptions of policing. Among the most influential factors, the global COVID-19 pandemic drastically altered workforce dynamics, prompting potential recruits to prioritize workplace flexibility, autonomy, and overall well-being. These shifts have impacted law enforcement particularly hard, as policing, by nature, is a high-stakes, highly visible field that hasn't been able to introduce the type of workplace flexibility seen in the private sector during and in the years following the pandemic.

The pandemic's influence has also accelerated a broader generational shift in workplace values, especially as younger Americans redefine work-life balance. Many in this generation have moved away from the previous "live to work" mentality that guided their parents and are instead advocating for a "work to live" approach, where personal fulfillment and well-being are given precedence over career advancement. With an increased focus on mental health, career satisfaction, and sustainable work environments, younger generations often seek professions that align more closely with these values. As a result, law enforcement agencies are struggling to attract recruits who are not only willing to engage in the demanding and oftentimes rigorous nature of police work but who are also open to the public scrutiny that comes with it. This generational shift, coupled with a widespread reassessment of career priorities, presents a significant challenge to law enforcement agencies already facing severe staffing shortages.

Additionally, the death of George Floyd on May 25, 2020, sparked global protests and widespread demands for police reform, fundamentally altering the public's perception of law enforcement. Calls for "defunding the police" grew louder, placing intense scrutiny on police practices and amplifying the demand for accountability and transparency in law enforcement.

This public response fueled widespread discussions about policing methods, resource allocation, and the role of police within communities, often portraying law enforcement in a critical light. As these conversations became more mainstream, the image of law enforcement as a stable and desirable career path suffered, leading to new challenges for departments attempting to recruit and retain officers. For many potential candidates, these shifts in public perception have raised questions about the future of the profession and the level of community support they would receive.

The effects of this cultural shift have created a challenging environment for law enforcement recruitment. Prospective recruits, especially those from younger generations, are often hesitant to join a field where negative perceptions are prevalent and where they may face social pressures or even resistance from their communities. In addition, heightened scrutiny has left many officers and would-be officers feeling that their efforts may be underappreciated, with some fearing that they may face blame and even criminal prosecution in an increasingly polarized environment. Together, these factors have compounded the existing vacancy crisis, as individuals who might have once been drawn to law enforcement are now turning to other careers with lower levels of public scrutiny and greater perceived stability, making it difficult for agencies to fill their ranks.

The gravity of the current law enforcement crisis is exacerbated by the aging workforce. Following the September 11, 2001 terrorist attacks, significant funding was allocated to increase law enforcement staffing and resources at the local, state, and federal levels. The creation of the Department of Homeland Security in 2002 and the subsequent influx of federal grants resulted in a significant increase in hiring for law enforcement agencies across the country. Now, more than two decades later, many of the candidates hired during that time are approaching retirement, posing a new challenge for agencies already struggling with recruitment and retention. As these experienced officers prepare to leave the profession, a lack of qualified candidates worsens an already dire situation, endangering both the future of law enforcement and the safety of the communities they serve.

Compounding this issue is the staggering rate at which younger officers are leaving law enforcement, often within just a few years of service. Many of these new officers enter the field with a sense of purpose and a desire to make a difference, only to find themselves disillusioned by the harsh realities of the job, including the physical and emotional toll, the increasing public scrutiny, and the sometimes contentious relationship between law enforcement and the communities they serve. This exodus reflects a broader cultural shift, where younger generations prioritize careers that align with their personal values, offer meaningful work-life balance, and provide a sense of fulfillment. Unlike their parents, who often stayed with one organization for decades, this generation is unafraid to seek new paths, making bold career transitions to pursue a life and purpose that genuinely resonates with them.

As these officers resign from the profession, their departure leaves a substantial gap in experience that intensifies the recruitment crisis and impedes the ability of agencies to properly mentor and prepare the next generation of law enforcement professionals. In many cases, officers with as little as three years of experience are being thrust into the role of Field Training Officers (FTOs), responsible for training and mentoring new recruits. Traditionally, these critical roles were reserved for more seasoned officers with a wealth of experience to share. Staffing shortages have forced agencies to rely on relatively inexperienced officers to fulfill these duties. The loss of officers with less than ten years of experience not only weakens the overall stability of law enforcement institutions but also poses a serious threat to the future of public safety.

The topic of police officer vacancies is not just a concern for law enforcement leaders; it's a matter that should concern every American. The dwindling number of police officers profoundly impacts public safety and community relations. Fewer officers mean longer response times, which can have dire consequences. National Public

Radio (NPR) reported that in New Orleans, the average response time for law enforcement tripled from 51 minutes in 2019 to a staggering 146 minutes in 2022. The Seattle City Council stated that the response time for certain crimes in their city could exceed 60 minutes following an exodus of 300 officers in 2020. These are not isolated examples but a troubling nationwide trend. In critical moments, those extra minutes could be the difference between a home invader being arrested or escaping, a loved one receiving timely medical attention or losing their life, or a drunk driver being stopped and arrested before hitting and killing a family in another vehicle. This is truly a life-and-death topic.

Fewer officers on the streets can also significantly impact the relationships built between law enforcement agencies and the people they serve. Community policing, the proactive strategy that builds trusting ties between law enforcement and their communities through collaborative efforts to address the causes of crime and disorder, relies on regular, consistent interactions between officers and citizens. The presence of officers in neighborhoods and communities is vital for fostering trust and maintaining effective policing.

Many law enforcement agencies have specialized units dedicated to improving community relations, but these are frequently the first to suffer personnel and budget cuts when staffing shortages occur. During my law enforcement career, I had the opportunity to work as a Community Resource Deputy, which focused on building trust and fostering positive relationships between community members and our sheriff's office. When I took over this position in 2019, there were ten deputies assigned to the unit, allowing us to be very active in the community and address quality-of-life issues effectively. We frequently led the agency in key areas such as arrests, traffic citations, and community event attendance, demonstrating our impact and importance to both the agency and the community we served.

As our agency's vacancies remained manageable, there was even talk of expanding the unit to meet growing needs. However,in 2024, as the agency's vacancies have increased, the number of deputies

COLIN WHITTINGTON

assigned to the Community Resource Unit dwindled to just four. This decrease reflects a broader trend across the country, where law enforcement leaders, facing limited resources and prioritizing immediate response demands, are compelled to reassign community officers to emergency response roles.

High vacancy rates also place an enormous burden on already overextended police officers, who are now responsible for covering areas meant to be patrolled by two or three officers. In some departments, the crisis has become so severe that officers face a relentless stream of calls from the moment they start their shift until they finally log off duty, leaving little time for report writing or even taking breaks. Oftentimes, officers are held out late to assist with additional calls for service, turning ten- or twelve-hour shifts into grueling marathons of work with another shift just hours away.

The most commonly cited reasons officers leave the profession before reaching the typical retirement age are long hours and overwhelming workloads. Chronic understaffing, coupled with the additional burden it brings, is a significant factor contributing to low morale and burnout issues in agencies nationwide. This creates a vicious cycle. As staffing levels drop, morale deteriorates further, prompting even more officers to leave, which in turn exacerbates the staffing and morale crisis.

Law enforcement is at a critical crossroads, where reversing the current downward spiral will demand sustained effort and a forward-thinking and modern approach to recruitment and retention. Historically, the profession has been slow to adapt, often resistant to embracing new ideas and strategies. Many agencies continue to rely on outdated methods that may have been successful in staffing their departments in the 20th century but are now ineffective in connecting with the younger generation of Americans. In response to the crisis, agencies nationwide have resorted to offering substantial sign-on bonuses, some as high as $100,000. These financial incentives have yielded mixed results, and their long-term impact on retention remains to be seen.

What can law enforcement agencies do to address the staffing crisis? How can they connect with their target audience, Millennials and Gen Z, and what message will resonate with them? Finally, how can agencies strike a balance between offering incentives to new recruits and maintaining the morale of current employees who may be dissatisfied with seeing rookie officers receive financial benefits that they were never given? These significant challenges must be tackled to secure the future of the Thin Blue Line.

Throughout most of my life, I knew I wanted to either join the military or enter the law enforcement profession. The idea of a job where I would spend all day sitting behind a desk sounded like a terrible form of torture to me. I craved excitement, variety, and the opportunity to make a meaningful impact in my community and my country. Little did I realize that my decision to pursue a career in law enforcement would not only satisfy my yearning for a dynamic and fulfilling profession but also serve as a springboard for my entrepreneurial ambitions beyond the badge. This journey ultimately inspired me to establish my own business, dedicated to assisting law enforcement officers and veterans as they transition to the private sector and supporting agencies in their recruitment and hiring efforts. Additionally, it paved the way for me to become a best-selling author with my debut book, "Beyond the Thin Blue Line."

In early 2015, my then-girlfriend, now wife, Shelby, told me about a Deputy Sheriff job opening with the Loudoun County Sheriff's Office in northern Virginia. Excited, I rushed to the agency's website to learn more. The department's website at the time was pretty limited regarding information most important to potential candidates. However, I could ascertain enough information to know I wanted to apply. I was surprised to learn that the agency's application needed to be printed, completed, and mailed in. There was no option to submit a digital application. As a Millennial accustomed to the convenience of online processes, this struck me as outdated, especially for the largest Sheriff's Office in Virginia, located in one of the wealthiest counties in America. I bring this up not as a complaint but to highlight how even well-funded organizations can sometimes lag in embracing digital transformation, particularly in their recruiting processes.

Over the next few months, I went through the agency's rigorous background process. I was assigned a fantastic investigator who was incredibly knowledgeable and helpful and genuinely wanted to see me succeed. Ironically, several years later, I became that investigator's supervisor! During the background investigation, I completed the physical abilities assessment, panel interview, background interview, polygraph, psychological exam, and medical exam. In total, my background process took approximately four months. Having successfully completed all portions of the background process, I was scheduled to interview with Sheriff Mike Chapman, the Sheriff of Loudoun County.

In early May 2015, I donned a suit and tie and reported to the Loudoun County Sheriff's Office Headquarters in Leesburg, Virginia. Sitting in the waiting room outside Sheriff Chapman's office, I reflected on the monumental decision I was about to make. I was a little nervous, but more than anything, I was excited. When Sheriff Chapman invited me into his office, I felt an unexpected sense of calm. This was the step I had envisioned for most of my life. During the interview, Sheriff Chapman inquired about my background, knowledge of the agency, and why I was drawn to this line of work. He also took the time to explain his vision for the agency and his expectations for his deputies. I was impressed that the leader of a nearly 900-person agency took the time to interview every deputy before they were hired. It was clear that Sheriff Chapman understood and valued the importance of hiring the right people to serve as sworn law enforcement officers. Thankfully, I met his expectations and was offered the position of Patrol Deputy.

My seven and a half years in law enforcement flew by while simultaneously seeming like the most significant years of my life. I started my career working on patrol in various parts of Loudoun County. I had the opportunity to respond to many significant calls for service, from simple larcenies to horrific homicides and suicides, while working alongside fantastic deputies, many of whom became lifelong friends. While working on patrol, I experienced the feeling of low staffing and its impact on me and my entire squad. Each deputy was frequently required to cover two or three sectors at a time, stay out late, or come in on a day off to assist another shift with their staffing.

After several years on patrol, I had the opportunity to serve in two specialty units, Community Policing and the Public Information Office. As a Community Policing Deputy, I witnessed firsthand law enforcement's profound impact on its community. Given the right resources and time, officers can forge deep, trusting bonds with the citizens they serve, fostering a sense of security and mutual respect. As the agency's Public Information Officer, I gained a deep appreciation for the importance of open and transparent communication between law enforcement agencies and the public. Clear, honest dialogue is crucial for building and maintaining community trust while also aiding the agency's recruiting efforts.

Without a doubt, 2019 was one of the most memorable years of my career. Early one April morning, I received an unexpected email from the Colonel, my agency's second-highest-ranking member, instructing me to attend the daily Command Staff meeting. I went to the Sheriff's conference room, wondering what I could have done to get called to a meeting that was usually only attended by the most senior agency members. To my great surprise, the agency's leadership team informed me that I had been named the 2019 Deputy Sheriff of the Year by the Virginia Sheriff's Association. Being named the deputy of the year from over 10,000 fantastic deputies in the state was an honor I'll never forget. A few months later, still brimming with excitement from this award, I tested for and was promoted to Sergeant. I was placed in charge of the agency's Employment Services Section, which recruits and conducts background checks on all new hires.

My time in recruiting and backgrounds was marked by many successes and some historic challenges. As a newly promoted Sergeant with no prior leadership experience, I was tasked with leading a unit with the critical mission of ensuring a steady stream of new deputies and civilian staff members for a nearly 900-person agency. I was thrust into a unit of seasoned background investigators, some with decades of law enforcement experience. Although I had no experience in recruiting or background investigations, I embraced the situation. I told my team I would rely on their expertise as I settled into my new role. Together, we quickly developed innovative initiatives to increase the number of applications and streamline the background process. I was eager and ready to make a difference.

Mike Tyson famously stated, "Everyone has a plan until they get punched in the face." Well, within just a few weeks into my new role, the world was thrown into the COVID-19 pandemic. The streets were deserted, job fairs were canceled, and a temporary hiring freeze was implemented for most of my agency's positions. Several months later, the law enforcement profession came under intense scrutiny following the death of George Floyd. Agencies across the country, already struggling with recruitment, were now facing an entirely new era in law enforcement. The cultural shift that followed these two historic events left many departments unprepared to address the mass exodus of officers and the subsequent recruitment challenges that emerged.

In the following months, police departments nationwide faced an unprecedented wave of officer resignations. Agencies in major metropolitan areas were hit particularly hard, with some losing dozens or even hundreds of officers. The resulting vacancies left departments scrambling to meet the growing demand for hiring new officers, often with far fewer applicants in the pipeline than needed. Despite these challenges, my team and I devised innovative recruiting strategies that helped us weather the storm and allowed our agency to achieve its lowest vacancy rate in decades by December 2020.

We recognized the need to appeal to the next generation of law enforcement professionals, understanding that traditional recruitment methods were no longer sufficient to address the growing need for law enforcement officers. Our approach involved broadening our reach beyond the local area and targeting potential candidates from across the country. We developed a dedicated recruiting website, launched a LinkedIn page specifically for recruitment, and leveraged social media advertising to connect with a broader audience. Additionally, we hosted virtual recruiting events, which proved to be a game-changer in reaching candidates who might not have otherwise considered our agency. We flew a 50-foot banner over several East Coast beaches, displayed billboards on major highways, put up recruiting banners in an international airport, and many other unique recruiting initiatives. These efforts brought in a wave of fantastic candidates and set a new standard for how law enforcement agencies can successfully adapt to changing times. I'll explore many of these strategies throughout this book, sharing insights that can benefit your department.

By 2022, like so many other officers, I realized that I no longer wanted to stay in law enforcement. Though I had thoroughly enjoyed my time as a deputy sheriff, a combination of factors led me to reconsider my future in uniform.Financial concerns, the relentless demands of the job, and growing frustrations with the bureaucratic hurdles common in local law enforcement were all contributing factors.

These frustrations are not mine alone; they are shared by law enforcement officers across the profession. These concerns are often overlooked by agencies that prioritize recruitment over retention, viewing the influx of new officers as the primary solution to staffing challenges.

However, this narrow focus can be profoundly detrimental. By concentrating primarily on recruitment, agencies risk neglecting the very individuals who have already invested years of loyal service with their departments. This oversight not only undermines the morale of existing officers but also erodes the overall stability and effectiveness of the law enforcement profession. When officers feel undervalued and unsupported, their dedication to the job diminishes, leading to a weakened workforce that is less equipped to handle the complexities of modern policing. Agencies must recognize the interconnectedness of recruitment and retention, understanding that one cannot be successful without the other.

Many law enforcement officers reach a pivotal moment in their careers between the 5-to-12-year mark, when they must weigh the decision to continue in their roles or embark on a new path. By this stage, they are typically seasoned professionals, having gained valuable experience and a comprehensive understanding of both the demands and rewards of the job. However, they may not yet be fully vested in their agency's retirement system, allowing them the flexibility to leave without facing significant financial repercussions. This can make it easier for them to consider departure, particularly if they feel disillusioned by a lack of support, limited opportunities for career advancement, or insufficient work-life balance.

As I approached my eighth year in law enforcement, I found myself at a crossroads where I needed to make that pivotal decision. I was entering a critical juncture in my career where I would soon be so deeply invested in my agency's retirement system that it would become increasingly impractical to leave. This realization prompted me to reflect deeply on my career aspirations and personal values, forcing me to consider what truly mattered to me. Ultimately, I chose to embrace a new experience in the private sector.

Unfortunately, my decision to leave law enforcement mirrors the experiences of countless officers nationwide who have served between five and twelve years. In my new business, I speak with officers from this demographic of law enforcement officers on a daily basis, and I frequently hear common themes in these conversations: many believe their agencies could have easily retained them with just a few proactive measures. These candid conversations have fueled my passion for advocating for enhanced retention strategies within the law enforcement profession. I am committed to helping agencies create an environment where officers feel valued, supported, and motivated. Recognizing that such an atmosphere is essential for the longevity and effectiveness of the law enforcement profession, I aim to champion these changes. By doing so, I hope to contribute to building a more resilient and dedicated workforce, ensuring that those who choose to serve can do so with pride and purpose.

The decision to stay or leave becomes pivotal for the individual officer and the agency as a whole. When officers in this mid-career phase choose to depart, it creates a challenging gap to fill; the loss of their experience and expertise reverberates throughout the department. This troubling trend of officers exiting the profession just as they reach their prime years of service underscores the urgent need for agencies to reassess their retention strategies. By addressing these concerns, we can foster an environment that not only retains seasoned officers but also nurtures the next generation of law enforcement professionals.

To break this cycle of attrition, agencies must recognize that retention is just as critical, if not more so, than recruitment. Effective retention strategies require a proactive approach that focuses on keeping seasoned officers engaged, motivated, and committed to their roles. This is particularly important during the mid-career phase, where the potential loss of experienced officers can have a long-lasting impact on department morale, institutional knowledge, and community relations. Agencies must invest in programs that address the specific needs of officers at this stage, such as offering opportunities for career growth, providing mental health and wellness support, and fostering a positive and inclusive work environment. Retention is not just about keeping numbers up. It is about sustaining a dedicated and experienced workforce that can uphold the integrity and mission of law enforcement in the long term. By placing a greater emphasis on retention, agencies can create a more stable, resilient, and effective force better equipped to serve and protect their communities.

Recruitment alone cannot compensate for the loss of experienced officers who leave due to unresolved frustrations and unmet needs. My experience has shown me that addressing retention is not just a complementary effort to recruitment but a fundamental necessity. Without it, the cycle of attrition will continue, and agencies will find themselves in a perpetual state of recruitment without ever achieving their staffing goals.

Solving the retention problem requires a comprehensive approach that addresses the root causes of why officers leave. Work-life balance is often a significant concern, as law enforcement demands can take a heavy toll on personal lives, leading to burnout and dissatisfaction. Career development opportunities also play a crucial role; officers who feel their professional growth is stunted or unrecognized are more likely to seek fulfillment elsewhere. Fair compensation is another obvious factor. When officers believe their compensation does not reflect the risks and responsibilities they shoulder, their loyalty to the agency wanes. These issues are particularly pressing for those with 5-10 years of service, who are experienced enough to know their worth and are at a point in their careers where they can still transition to a new field without significant financial repercussions.

For law enforcement agencies to retain their most valuable asset, their people, they must tackle these challenges head-on. This means offering competitive salaries and benefits and creating an environment where officers feel supported, valued, and given opportunities to advance. Agencies must demonstrate a genuine commitment to their officers' well-being, both professionally and personally, if they hope to build a stable and effective force. By prioritizing retention with the same intensity as recruitment, agencies can break the cycle of attrition that has become a significant factor for most agencies throughout America.

In the years since leaving law enforcement, I have prioritized staying connected with the profession I hold dear and the dedicated individuals who serve on the Thin Blue Line. Several months after leaving the Loudoun County Sheriff's Office, I founded Recruiting Heroes LLC, a business committed to supporting law enforcement officers, veterans, and public safety agencies. We specialize in helping candidates prepare for their lives and careers after their years of service by providing resume writing, LinkedIn profile optimization, and career coaching services.

Our mission extends beyond helping veterans and first responders transition to the private sector; we also collaborate with law enforcement agencies nationwide to address their recruiting, hiring, and retention challenges. The strategies and insights shared throughout this book are the ones my team and I apply daily with our clients, aimed at strengthening the future of those who protect and serve our country. If your agency is struggling with your recruiting and retention efforts, Recruiting Heroes would love to help. I encourage you to visit our website, www.RecruitingHeroesLLC.com, to learn more.

In this book, I aim to share the insights and experiences I've gained from my years in law enforcement and private sector recruiting, bolstered by extensive interviews with exiting law enforcement officers. Throughout my career, I've witnessed firsthand the evolving challenges and complexities law enforcement agencies face in attracting and retaining top talent. My goal is to critically examine traditional recruiting efforts in law enforcement, highlighting why these methods are no longer sufficient in the 21st century.

The world has changed dramatically over the past few decades, and with it, so have the expectations and motivations of those entering the workforce. In this book, we will delve into the importance of targeting the right candidates, not just those who meet the basic qualifications but those who embody the qualities necessary for modern policing. We'll explore how community engagement plays a crucial role in effective recruitment and why agencies must actively build relationships within the communities they serve to identify and attract potential recruits.

In addition, I will offer my perspective on hiring bonuses, analyzing their potential advantages while also considering the risks they pose to agency cohesion and long-term retention. While hiring bonuses may provide a quick fix to staffing shortages, they can also create divisions within the department and fail to address underlying issues that contribute to turnover. It's essential to strike a balance between offering incentives and fostering a workplace environment that promotes loyalty and career satisfaction.

We'll also explore the generational differences that significantly influence career choices and job satisfaction, particularly among Millennials and Generation Z. As law enforcement agencies face the challenge of recruiting and retaining younger candidates, it's crucial to align organizational culture with the values and expectations of these generations. For example, Millennials and Gen Z often prioritize work-life balance, career growth, and meaningful work over traditional notions of job security and status. This book emphasizes the importance of these factors. It provides actionable insights on how agencies can adapt to appeal to a new generation of recruits while staying true to their core mission and values.

Moreover, this book outlines a comprehensive approach to enhancing your agency's recruiting and retention strategies, focusing on building a resilient workforce capable of adapting to the evolving demands of law enforcement. We'll delve into the pivotal role social media plays in modern recruiting, particularly how platforms like LinkedIn can be used to target ideal candidates and reach potential recruits around America. In today's digital age, social media offers unprecedented opportunities to connect with candidates who align with your agency's values and mission.

We will explore the shift from traditional to digital recruitment methods, including how to leverage online job platforms and social media campaigns to attract a broader and more diverse pool of candidates. Additionally, this book will cover how to utilize data and analytics to track the success of your recruiting efforts. By implementing data-driven strategies, agencies can measure the effectiveness of their campaigns, identify trends, and make informed decisions to optimize their approaches. This includes analyzing metrics such as application rates, candidate engagement, and the success rates of various recruiting channels.

Further, we'll discuss strategies for creating compelling content that resonates with prospective candidates and building a strong online presence that showcases your agency's culture, achievements, and community impact. We will also emphasize the importance of fostering job satisfaction through supportive work environments and strong leadership and the critical role of transparent and collaborative policing in building community trust. Together, these strategies will help your agency develop a more effective and sustainable recruitment and retention model.

Additionally, we'll explore the concept of turning every member of your agency into an unofficial recruiter as a key strategy for a successful, agency-wide recruiting push. By cultivating a culture where all employees engage actively in the recruitment process, agencies can access a wider network of potential candidates and strengthen their outreach efforts. This approach leverages the diverse networks and experiences of current staff members while also fostering a strong, unified team dedicated to the agency's mission and values.

Together, we will build a strategic vision for the future of law enforcement by developing sustainable recruitment and retention models that can help agencies thrive in an ever-changing landscape. These models will not only address immediate staffing needs but will also focus on long-term success by creating a positive work culture that values professional development, diversity, and community engagement.

I remain deeply committed to the success of the law enforcement profession and have been disheartened by the extreme difficulties agencies face in attracting and retaining staff. This profession, though incredibly challenging, is essential to maintaining a peaceful and democratic society. Law enforcement officers are the backbone of community safety, tasked with upholding the law and protecting citizens, often under complex and demanding conditions. The current struggles with recruitment and retention impact the immediate effectiveness of law enforcement agencies and the long-term stability and trust within our communities.

I hope that the topics discussed in this book will inspire police chiefs, sheriffs, law enforcement, and political leaders to rethink their recruitment and retention strategies. We must move beyond outdated practices and adopt modern approaches that align with the evolving needs of today's workforce. By exploring innovative strategies and incorporating data-driven insights, agencies can better attract and retain top talent. The goal is to create a dynamic and supportive environment that appeals to the next generation of law enforcement professionals and equips them to meet contemporary challenges with confidence and competence.

By embracing these new strategies and focusing on the core values and traditions that make law enforcement a noble and vital profession, we can ensure that the best and brightest candidates continue to join and strengthen the Thin Blue Line. Through this commitment to modernizing our approach and fostering a positive work culture, we will maintain the integrity and effectiveness of law enforcement agencies. Together, we can build a future where law enforcement professionals are not only well-equipped to face the demands of their roles but are also celebrated and supported in their crucial work

# CHAPTER TWO
# RETENTION, RETENTION, RETENTION

I suspect that most readers will approach this book with the belief that it will dive right into the topic of law enforcement recruitment, leaving retention strategies to the very end as a mere afterthought. That is certainly the case with many books covering recruitment and retention in other industries. However, I firmly believe that a truly effective law enforcement recruitment strategy begins with a strong foundation of retention and agency morale. Retention is far more critical than recruitment, and the failure of the law enforcement profession to focus on the morale and well-being of their current officers is the leading cause of the vacancy crisis we find ourselves in today.

Retention is the backbone of a strong and effective law enforcement agency. While recruitment grabs headlines and drives social media campaigns, retention ensures agencies maintain experienced officers who embody institutional knowledge, foster community trust, and mentor new recruits. Retaining officers goes beyond simply filling positions and holding on to officers; it's about cultivating an environment that encourages long-term commitment, professional satisfaction, and loyalty. Agencies that prioritize retention strategies not only save on recruitment costs but also enhance their operational effectiveness and public perception.

Too often, agencies focus almost exclusively on bringing in as many new candidates as possible while neglecting the exceptional officers already serving their communities. This shortsighted approach not only undervalues the contributions of experienced personnel but also fosters a revolving door effect, driving up costs, reducing operational efficiency, and eroding morale across the department. Retention is not merely a supplementary concern but the foundation upon which successful recruitment efforts must be built. After all, what is the point of attracting top talent if you can't keep them for the long term?

I often use the analogy of a water bucket to illustrate this point. You can pour in as much water (recruits) as you like, but if there's a gaping hole at the bottom of the bucket (your agency), the water will continuously flow out. No matter how much effort you put into filling the bucket, it will never stay full unless you first address the hole. Similarly, without a strong retention strategy, even the best recruitment campaigns will fail to create the lasting, sustainable workforce your agency needs.

Retention begins with understanding why officers leave and addressing those issues before they become breaking points. While the financial aspect is often attributed to why officers leave the profession, I have found that burnout, limited career progression, feelings of underappreciation, and lack of trust from senior leadership play far more significant roles in the serious retention problem law enforcement is experiencing. By implementing targeted retention strategies, ranging from fostering inclusivity and belonging to creating transparent promotional pathways, agencies can combat these challenges and build a workforce that feels valued and motivated to stay.

Much like recruitment, retention requires intentionality and consistency. Agencies must actively invest in their officers by providing meaningful opportunities for growth, recognition, and connection. When officers feel that their contributions matter and that they have a future within the department, they are more likely to remain engaged and committed to the agency's mission.

At its core, retention isn't just about keeping numbers up; it's about preserving the true heart of law enforcement. Its people. Officers who stay become the pillars of their departments, upholding standards, fostering camaraderie, and exemplifying the values of service and integrity. By building a culture that prioritizes loyalty and longevity, agencies can ensure their officers remain with their department and continuously grow and thrive throughout their careers.

This chapter explores strategies to address retention challenges head-on, offering actionable insights to help agencies create an environment where officers want to stay, grow, and excel. From strengthening leadership engagement to addressing promotional transparency and supporting mid-career officers, the following pages outline a roadmap for cultivating loyalty, stability, and excellence within every department. While being self-critical and aware of one's shortcomings is far from easy, only agencies willing to acknowledge their faults and actively work to improve them stand a chance at enhancing officer retention. Meanwhile, agencies led by unyielding executives will continue to see their officers transfer to other departments or leave the profession entirely.

## WHY DO OFFICERS LEAVE?

There's no doubt that losing officers, especially those who leave before reaching retirement age, has a profound and disruptive impact on organizations. Critical positions become vacant, often suddenly and unexpectedly, disrupting operations and straining resources. The departure of a valued teammate affects not only workflow but also morale, as colleagues must adapt to the loss of someone who likely contributed to a positive work environment. Furthermore, these departures can spark a ripple effect, causing others within the agency to question their own career paths or explore alternative opportunities after witnessing their coworkers leave.

Beyond the operational challenges, the financial toll of high turnover rates is significant. Have you or your team ever calculated the true cost of recruiting, hiring, and training a new officer? Factor in the expenses of overtime pay to cover the vacancy, recruiter salaries, background investigations, instructor hours, training programs, equipment, and other associated costs. For many departments, these combined expenses can quickly surpass $100,000 per new hire, highlighting the urgent need to prioritize retention and minimize turnover.

To have any hope of addressing the root causes of retention challenges in law enforcement, we must first understand why officers are leaving the profession. In my new career, I have had the opportunity to speak with thousands of law enforcement professionals considering leaving a job they once loved and dreamed about since they were kids. When first starting my business, I assumed that I would primarily help officers who had reached retirement age and were looking for their next job after a distinguished career in law enforcement. However, I was surprised to find that over 60% of the candidates I work with have just 5-12 years on the job and are looking to get out of the profession early. Many are regular patrol officers, while others are detectives, sergeants, lieutenants, and even higher-ranking members of departments across the country. What is causing these officers to leave midway through their careers as they are just starting to hit their stride in their profession?

Burnout is a silent yet relentless force and is one of the most prevalent reasons given to me for why officers are walking away from the badge. It is far more than simply feeling tired after a long shift. Burnout manifests as emotional exhaustion, chronic stress, and a creeping sense of detachment from the job, often exacerbated by the high-stakes and relentless nature of police work. Over time, burnout can rob officers of their passion and drive, leaving them disillusioned and searching for an escape. If unaddressed, this phenomenon becomes a powerful force pushing experienced officers out of the profession entirely.

Burnout played a significant role in my decision to leave law enforcement. As is so often the case in organizations, strong performers are often "rewarded" for their efforts with even more work, while less effective employees are allowed to skate by and are given fewer and fewer responsibilities. By the time I resigned from my agency, I was not only supervising the entire recruiting and background investigation unit, but I was also tasked with serving as one of the agency's public information officers, assisting with training and onboarding, serving on several agency committees, and more. Although I found many of these tasks fulfilling and willingly took them on, I failed to recognize the immense weight I was carrying until the burnout had fully set in. This experience is far too common among officers nationwide. Driven by an unwavering commitment to excellence and a fear of disappointing their leadership, many accept more and more responsibilities, unaware that they are paving a path that may ultimately lead them to leave the profession altogether. Departments must do more to recognize and combat burnout, providing mental health resources, peer support programs, and structural changes that mitigate stressors before they become overwhelming.

Another significant factor driving officers out of the profession is the pervasive lack of trust and support many feel from their leadership teams. In countless conversations with officers contemplating leaving law enforcement, many expressed the belief that their leaders care more about optics and politics than protecting and supporting their team.

This perception stems from various sources. Some officers feel that when faced with public criticism or internal controversies, leadership is quick to blame individual officers rather than standing by their team and examining the systemic factors that may have contributed to the issue. In such moments, many officers describe feeling "thrown under the bus," as if their hard work, sacrifices, and years of service are overshadowed by a single incident or the fear of public backlash.

Additionally, the lack of open communication and transparency from leadership can amplify these feelings of mistrust. Decisions that directly impact officers' lives, such as schedule changes, staffing levels, or disciplinary actions, are sometimes made without seeking input from those on the front lines. This top-down approach to management leaves officers feeling like mere cogs in a machine rather than valued members of the organization.

Compounding the problem, many officers report that their concerns about safety, workload, and career development are either ignored or met with hollow promises. When leaders fail to follow through on commitments or appear disconnected from the realities of patrol work, morale plummets. Officers begin to feel that they are unsupported and expendable. This erosion of trust doesn't just hurt individual officers. It damages entire organizations. Officers who feel unsupported and undervalued are less likely to go above and beyond in their duties, less engaged with their work, and more likely to seek opportunities elsewhere.

To rebuild trust and foster a culture of mutual respect, law enforcement leaders must take proactive steps to show their officers that they are valued and supported. This starts with accountability at all levels, ensuring that leaders are as willing to take responsibility for failures as they are to celebrate successes. It also requires genuine two-way communication, where officers feel safe sharing their concerns and know their voices are being heard.

Furthermore, leaders must stand by their officers in challenging times, advocating for them when they make honest mistakes and addressing systemic issues that contribute to problems rather than scapegoating individuals. Building trust is not about avoiding criticism or controversy but demonstrating integrity, fairness, and a commitment to the well-being of those who put their lives on the line every day.

Financial concerns also play a significant role in the current exodus of law enforcement officers. Despite the risks and responsibilities associated with the profession, many officers feel their compensation does not adequately reflect their sacrifices. Rising living costs, stagnant salaries, and limited benefits packages can push officers to reconsider their commitment to law enforcement, especially when alternative industries offer more competitive pay and greater work-life balance. Departments must assess whether their compensation packages are keeping pace with industry standards and the financial realities of their officers.

Officers' demanding and often unpredictable schedules add another layer of complexity. Long hours, rotating shifts, and missed family milestones can strain personal relationships and erode job satisfaction. It is no surprise that law enforcement officers have significantly higher divorce rates than the general public. While operational needs may necessitate these schedules, agencies that fail to explore flexible scheduling or time-off policies risk alienating their workforce. Finding creative solutions to scheduling challenges can show officers that their well-being is valued and prioritized.

Another significant factor is the lack of career growth opportunities. Officers often leave because they see no clear path to advance their careers within their current department. Without transparent promotional criteria, mentorship opportunities, or access to specialized training, officers may feel stagnated. Agencies should focus on creating pathways for professional development, ensuring that officers can envision a long-term future within the department.

Equally important is fostering open dialogue between leadership and staff. Officers need to feel that their voices are heard and their concerns taken seriously. Regular roll call briefings, surveys, and informal check-ins provide platforms for officers to express their needs and frustrations, enabling leadership to address issues proactively. Building a culture of communication and trust can help agencies identify and resolve problems before they escalate into reasons for departure.

Exit interviews are another invaluable tool for understanding why officers choose to leave. While it is too late to retain those leaving the organization, these interviews can offer critical insights into systemic issues that might otherwise go unnoticed. Agencies should approach exit interviews as opportunities for constructive feedback, asking departing officers what changes could have kept them in the team and using this information to improve policies and practices to prevent others from wanting to leave.

Retention strategies must also extend to addressing mid-career challenges. Officers often face a crossroads in their careers, where the initial excitement has faded, and long-term rewards seem distant. Recognizing and addressing the unique needs of mid-career officers through targeted incentives, leadership opportunities, and peer support programs can help retain this vital segment of the workforce.

Ultimately, agencies that invest in understanding and addressing why officers leave will be better positioned to retain their talent. Retention is not about creating a one-size-fits-all solution but rather about recognizing the diverse needs and challenges officers face at different stages of their careers. By fostering a supportive, transparent, and growth-oriented environment, law enforcement agencies can reduce turnover, strengthen morale, and build a resilient, loyal workforce committed to serving their communities.

## FIX THE LEAK

Retention shouldn't just be a strategy; it's a cultural shift. For agencies to keep their officers long-term, they must recognize that retention starts on day one, not when officers first begin voicing their frustrations or handing in their resignation memorandums. A commitment to retention is a commitment to the well-being and professional development of every officer in your department. It must be embedded in your agency's DNA and become a primary focus for your entire agency. Like all law enforcement departments, your team probably has exciting plans to implement innovative programs, build community relations, and reduce crime rates in your

COLIN WHITTINGTON

jurisdiction. None of these things are possible if you are constantly struggling with significant vacancies that require you to direct your resources to simply respond to calls for service.

Leadership is the foundation upon which any successful retention effort is built. Supervisors, managers, and command staff wield enormous influence in shaping a department's culture and officers' experiences. When leaders create an environment of support, trust, and engagement, officers are more likely to remain loyal, motivated, and invested in their roles. Conversely, toxic leadership, indifference, or a lack of visibility can drive even the most dedicated officers to seek opportunities elsewhere.

Chiefs, sheriffs, and command staff members are the architects of departmental culture. Their actions, or inactions, reverberate throughout the organization, affecting morale and retention. Effective leaders prioritize being visible, approachable, and engaged with every member of their team, regardless of rank. Unfortunately, many law enforcement officers I work with tell me they have not seen their senior leadership team in months. Some admit that they've never met the chief or sheriff of their department. This level of detachment is unacceptable, regardless of the agency's size.

Senior leaders must regularly connect and interact with their teams. This means attending roll calls, participating in ride-alongs, and engaging in meaningful conversations with officers. These interactions are opportunities to communicate the organization's vision, show support for the officers' efforts, and share updates on initiatives aimed at improving their work environment. When officers hear directly from their leaders and feel valued for their contributions, they develop a stronger sense of purpose and belonging within the department.

Engagement is a two-way street. It is not enough for leaders to speak to their officers; they must also listen. An officer who feels heard and appreciated is far more likely to stay with the organization than one who believes their voice doesn't matter. Leaders must create an atmosphere where feedback and suggestions are encouraged and welcomed without fear of retribution or dismissal. If leaders respond with anger or indifference to ideas or concerns, they risk fostering a culture of silence, where officers no longer feel safe to speak candidly. If a chief or sheriff asks for feedback or questions during a roll call or meeting and is met with silence, chances are they have not yet established a trusting environment where officers feel comfortable speaking up. Leaders must consistently demonstrate that they are open to feedback and genuinely interested in what their team has to say.

Imagine the profound impact on morale and engagement when an idea from a patrol officer or deputy is carefully considered, researched, and implemented. The officer who proposed the idea will feel immense pride and validation, knowing their contribution made a tangible difference and that their idea has become a policy or practice within the agency. This success, in turn, inspires others to share their ideas and feedback, creating a ripple effect of empowerment across the organization. Not only will you drastically increase the buy-in from your staff, leading to better retention rates, but you will likely also receive many fantastic ideas from those currently doing the job and experiencing shortcomings in the department, which these ideas can address.

Building this kind of environment requires sustained effort and dedication from the leadership team. Leaders must actively seek opportunities to gather input from their officers, not just during promotional interviews or annual surveys, but as an ongoing practice. Regularly soliciting feedback reinforces the message that every team member's perspective is valued and that leadership is committed to continuous improvement.

It's important to acknowledge that not every idea or suggestion can be implemented. Budget constraints, regulations, and other external factors may limit what is feasible. However, officers understand these realities. While they may be frustrated at times, most officers realize the position their leadership team is in and that not every idea can easily be implemented. However, what they value most is the opportunity to express their ideas in an environment of honesty, respect, and transparency. They want to know their voices are heard and that leadership appreciates their willingness to contribute, even if the answer to a specific proposal is "not right now" or "not possible." However, you must give feedback and explain the reasoning behind the decision against an idea. Officer frustration occurs when their ideas are shot down without any explanation.

Beyond listening to feedback, law enforcement leaders must consistently demonstrate their faith in their officers through their actions. Words alone are not enough; leaders must show that they genuinely support their teams, even in challenging situations. Officers who feel valued and trusted are likelier to remain committed to their agencies and perform at their best. Conversely, nothing erodes morale faster than a leader who prematurely assigns blame or publicly undermines their officers.

Mistakes are inevitable in law enforcement, and instances of misconduct must be addressed appropriately. However, significant issues arise when assumptions are made before a fair and thorough investigation is conducted. When agency leaders speak negatively about their officers to the media or outside entities without knowing the whole story, it creates a culture of distrust and fear. Officers begin to feel unsupported, as though their leadership prioritizes public opinion over the well-being of their people. This doesn't just affect the officers involved in a specific incident; it sends a ripple effect through the entire department, lowering morale across the board.

Public comments from chiefs or sheriffs about officer mistakes, sometimes made within hours of an event, can have devastating consequences. Often intended to appease public criticism, these statements can lead to widespread disillusionment within the ranks. Officers may feel alienated from their leadership, agency, and community. This sense of betrayal often contributes to mass resignations or retirements, creating retention crises in departments already struggling to maintain adequate staffing.

In the immediate aftermath of a significant incident, such as an officer-involved shooting, accidental discharge, or officer arrest, leaders need to demonstrate unwavering support for their department. This begins with clear communication, emphasizing a commitment to fairness and thoroughness in investigations. Leaders should reassure their teams that no sweeping assumptions will be made and decisions will be based on facts rather than external pressures.

Equally important is the approach to public communication. Leaders must prioritize internal processes, ensuring that all decisions and follow-ups are addressed within the agency before making statements to the public. Premature or poorly considered comments can jeopardize trust within the department and complicate the public narrative, leading to further scrutiny and demoralization.

Every word a leader speaks in these critical moments carries weight. Thoughtful, measured communication can reinforce confidence, preserve morale, and maintain trust throughout the agency. Conversely, missteps in messaging can have long-lasting impacts, affecting retention, performance, and the overall cohesion of the department. By choosing their words carefully and focusing on internal accountability, leaders can navigate these challenging situations while safeguarding their team's trust and stability.

To retain top talent, law enforcement leaders must prioritize the creation of a trusting, supportive, and feedback-driven culture. This requires visible and consistent efforts to engage with officers, celebrate their contributions, and ensure they feel valued and connected to the organization's mission. Retention is not about grand gestures or sporadic acts of engagement. It is about the everyday actions of leadership: walking the halls, joining the team on the streets, stopping to assist with a crash or disabled vehicle, and fostering a sense of camaraderie and trust. A culture where officers feel supported and heard is one where they will want to stay, grow, and contribute to the department's success for years to come.

While the actions of a department's most senior members undoubtedly shape the overall culture of a law enforcement agency, the officers' immediate supervisors have the most profound influence on morale and retention. An organization might be the most exceptional workplace in the world, but if an employee's immediate supervisor consistently tears them down, disregards their opinions, and makes their work life miserable, that employee will ultimately develop a negative view of the entire agency. A chief or sheriff can adopt a visionary, employee-first leadership style, but if their sergeants and lieutenants fail to reflect and embody those same values, the leader's vision will never take hold. The frontline supervisors are the bridge between leadership's goals and the boots-on-the-ground realities, making their role indispensable.

Therefore, selecting and promoting the right individuals for low- to mid-level supervisory roles is one of the most critical decisions any agency can make. When I interviewed for the sergeant position in my agency, I told my sheriff and colonel that I believed the sergeant role was the most critical in the entire organization. Most of an agency's workforce, its officers, detectives, and administrative staff, report directly to a sergeant. This means that sergeants are responsible for creating the daily work environment for the majority of employees in the organization. Whether that environment fosters growth, productivity, and teamwork or frustration, apathy, and division depends entirely on the quality of the supervisors. Selecting even one sergeant who seeks rank for selfish or misguided reasons can have disastrous ripple effects, poisoning morale and diminishing trust within their sphere of influence.

Frontline supervisors, particularly sergeants, are the cornerstone of any law enforcement agency. They set the tone for the rank-and-file workforce, directly influencing policies and how officers feel about their work. A good sergeant acts as a mentor, coach, and advocate, providing guidance while also holding their team accountable. They foster camaraderie and ensure officers under their command feel valued and supported. Conversely, a poor sergeant can be a barrier between officers and the organization, sowing discord and resentment through micromanagement, favoritism, or neglect.

Promotions to supervisory positions should not be based solely on tenure, technical skills, or personal connections. Agencies must prioritize character, emotional intelligence, and leadership potential. A good sergeant must inspire confidence, de-escalate conflicts, and make fair decisions under pressure. They should be approachable yet firm, embodying the agency's core values in every interaction. This requires a rigorous selection process, including in-depth interviews, performance evaluations, and feedback from peers and subordinates to identify candidates who genuinely have the organization's best interests at heart.

The influence of frontline supervisors extends far beyond their immediate team. A motivated and well-supported group of officers can elevate the entire agency's reputation, improving community trust and engagement. On the other hand, dysfunction at the supervisory level can erode public confidence, increase turnover, and make it difficult to attract high-quality recruits. This makes the role of sergeants not just important internally but critical to the agency's external success.

Even after promotion, agencies must remain committed to the continuous development of their supervisors. Leadership is not a static skill. It evolves with experience, reflection, and ongoing education. To meet the demands of modern policing, agencies should provide sergeants with access to leadership development programs, stress management resources, and opportunities for peer collaboration. New sergeants, in particular, need tailored support to thrive in their roles. Training should go beyond technical skills like report approvals, timesheets, and performance evaluations. It should serve as a roadmap for the type of leadership the agency values and expects.

Departments should encourage sergeants to read leadership books, attend courses on employee relations, and engage in self-assessment to refine their leadership philosophy. This approach helps them better understand how to motivate, support, and manage their teams effectively. Continuous growth enables sergeants to adapt to new challenges, foster stronger team relationships, and model the organization's values. And while you're at it, why not give every new sergeant a copy of this book? After all, it's a lot cheaper than hiring a consultant, and it fits nicely in a duty bag. A sergeant who is invested in their personal and professional development will be better equipped to inspire trust, drive performance, and create a positive workplace culture.

Senior leadership must actively support and empower frontline supervisors, recognizing that their success directly influences the morale and performance of the entire organization. This begins with maintaining open lines of communication, where supervisors feel heard, valued, and confident in sharing their challenges and insights. Leadership must also model the behaviors they wish to see at all levels of the agency, demonstrating fairness, accountability, and respect in every interaction.

Supervisors who feel genuinely supported by senior leaders are far more likely to extend that same support to their teams, fostering a culture of trust, collaboration, and shared purpose. Conversely, supervisors who feel undervalued, micromanaged, or ignored often mirror those negative behaviors with their subordinates, creating a ripple effect of dissatisfaction and disengagement throughout the workforce. By prioritizing empowerment over control and investing in the well-being and growth of frontline supervisors, senior leadership can cultivate a positive and cohesive organizational culture that drives long-term success.

## CREATING OPPORTUNITIES FOR GROWTH

A significant factor in officer retention is the availability of opportunities for career advancement and skill development. Law enforcement officers thrive when they can envision a future within their department. They want to work for an agency that offers challenges, rewards, and the chance to grow professionally. Whether through promotions, specialized assignments, or lateral career opportunities, providing clear pathways for advancement is essential to keeping officers engaged and motivated. Without these opportunities, many officers feel stagnant and may seek new challenges outside the department, leading to avoidable turnover.

Many officers who seek my company's assistance express a common sentiment: they feel they have "done all I can" within their agency. This sense of hitting a glass ceiling, where there's no clear path for advancement or growth, can significantly erode their investment in the organization. When employees feel stuck, their motivation wanes, often leading to performance-related issues, a decline in morale within their units, and, ultimately, their decision to leave the department altogether.

While it's unrealistic for an agency to meet every employee's desire for promotions or lateral moves, fostering a culture of transparency and opportunity is essential. Clear expectations about career progression, open communication about available opportunities, and fair, well-defined processes can make a significant difference. These practices keep employees engaged and show them that their contributions are valued and that the agency is committed to their professional growth. By addressing these concerns proactively, agencies can minimize the frustration and disengagement that often precede turnover, retaining a motivated and productive workforce.

Transparent and fair promotional processes are crucial to fostering trust and loyalty. Officers must believe their hard work, skills, and dedication will be fairly recognized and rewarded. Agencies must ensure that promotion criteria are clearly defined, that evaluation processes are impartial and that there is open communication about how decisions are made. Too often, I hear from employees who feel hard done by their department's promotional processes, believing that less-deserving officers were promoted over them. A lack of transparency in promotions can lead to frustration, rumors, and distrust, driving talented officers to seek opportunities elsewhere.

The promotional process in my agency required submitting a memorandum of interest, completing a multifaceted assessment, and interviewing with the sheriff and the colonel. The agency made commendable efforts to ensure the process was fair and unbiased. However, the results of the process were never disclosed to any of the participants. No one knew how they performed or how they ranked compared to their peers. Ultimately, promotions were decided entirely at the sheriff's discretion. Unsurprisingly, this lack of transparency fueled rumors and speculation, with some disgruntled employees blaming favoritism and an unfair selection process on their not being selected. Whether this was true or not was irrelevant to some staff members. The simple appearance of an unfair process is enough to send some employees spiraling into feelings of frustration and the desire to resign.

Adding to this frustration was the absence of clear communication regarding the timing of promotions or transfers. Surprise promotional announcements, often delivered at the very end of the day on a Friday, kept the entire agency in a constant state of uncertainty. This fostered a cycle of guesswork and rumors about when the next promotional or transfer memo would appear. Employees were constantly on edge, wondering what the next memo would say and what part of the agency they could be transferred to or promoted to.

While there are valid reasons for operating in this manner, law enforcement leadership must recognize the unintended consequences of such practices. Officers who perceive that they were unjustly overlooked for a promotion or transfer, whether that perception is accurate or not, often experience feelings of frustration and resentment. This can diminish their individual performance and negatively affect the morale of those around them.

To address these issues, agencies should prioritize transparency and communication in their promotional and transfer processes. Sharing assessment results, providing consistent participant feedback, and reducing secrecy can significantly reduce the backlash associated with these decisions. An open, honest, and transparent approach to promotions and transfers is essential for maintaining morale and fostering a culture of trust. Furthermore, it is critical in enhancing retention efforts, ensuring that employees feel valued and fairly treated.

Beyond promotions, professional development is a cornerstone of retention. Agencies should invest in programs that help officers enhance their skills and achieve their long-term goals. This includes offering tuition reimbursement for advanced education, access to leadership development courses, and workshops tailored to specific career tracks. Providing these resources demonstrates an agency's commitment to its workforce and underscores the value placed on its officers' growth.

Leadership training programs are another vital tool for retention. Preparing officers for supervisory roles helps agencies cultivate future leaders ready to take on greater responsibilities. Leadership programs should focus on developing skills like communication, conflict resolution, and strategic thinking while emphasizing the department's values and mission. When officers see that their agency is invested in preparing them for leadership, they are more likely to envision a long-term future within the organization.

Furthermore, agencies should encourage continuous learning and provide resources that align with officers' aspirations. Whether sending officers to conferences, arranging for guest speakers, or supporting certifications in specialized fields, these opportunities signal that the department values the professional growth of its employees. Officers who feel supported in their career journeys are more likely to stay engaged and committed, viewing their agency as a partner in their success.

Finally, creating a culture that prioritizes growth benefits the officers and the entire department. When officers have opportunities to expand their skills and advance their careers, the agency benefits from a more knowledgeable, adaptable, and satisfied workforce. This mutual investment fosters loyalty, reduces turnover, and strengthens the department's overall performance. By prioritizing career advancement and development, agencies can build a motivated team dedicated to serving their communities for the long term.

## SUPPORTING OFFICERS BEYOND THE BADGE

Developing programs and processes to help officers prepare for retirement and their subsequent careers is a powerful and surprising way to enhance employee satisfaction and demonstrate that leadership truly cares about their well-being. Every officer in your agency will eventually transition out of law enforcement. It is an inevitable reality of the profession. Much like the military's Transition Assistance Program, I believe it is our duty to help officers prepare for life and career opportunities beyond their law enforcement service.

I created a half-day course titled Beyond the Thin Blue Line: Career Strategies for Law Enforcement Officers to address this need. This course is designed to equip officers with essential skills, including identifying industries of interest, crafting compelling resumes, understanding the power of networking, mastering interview techniques, and more. I am always surprised by the number of agencies that tell me they do not wish to teach their officers these skills out of fear of losing them to other professions. Rightfully so, officer wellness has become a greater topic over the past decade. However, can we really claim to care about our officers if we only care about them while they are filling a position in our agency? Shouldn't we care about their well-being for the rest of their lives, not just while they provide a service to us? True leadership prioritizes their welfare not just while they are serving but for the rest of their lives.

Courses like *Beyond the Thin Blue Line* instill confidence in officers about their futures, enabling them to remain fully engaged in their law enforcement careers until the day they retire.

Furthermore, offering such programs can be a unique and compelling recruitment tool. Imagine a candidate evaluating potential agencies. She notices that your department offers a comprehensive career transition program, signaling a deep commitment to its employees' long-term success and well-being. This candidate is far more likely to choose an agency that demonstrates it values its people as whole individuals, not just as employees.

If you are interested in hosting *Beyond the Thin Blue Line* at your agency, visit RecruitingHeroesLLC.com for more information or to schedule a session. I've had the privilege of traveling across the country and around the globe to teach this vital course and share its message. It would be an honor to bring it to your department and help your officers prepare for a future they can approach with confidence and excitement. By investing in their long-term success, you support their well-being and strengthen your agency's reputation as a forward-thinking, people-centered organization.

## ADDRESSING BURNOUT AND CULTIVATING WORK-LIFE BALANCE

Burnout is one of the most pressing challenges facing the law enforcement profession today. The relentless demands of police work, long hours, high stress, and repeated exposure to emotionally taxing situations can significantly impact an officer's mental, emotional, and physical health. If left unaddressed, burnout diminishes individual well-being and performance and leads to the loss of seasoned officers. For agencies, this means forfeiting valuable institutional knowledge and expertise, further straining their ability to serve their communities effectively.

One of the most common but counterproductive practices in law enforcement is imposing undue burdens on high-performing officers. These individuals often take on additional responsibilities because they are committed to their jobs and do not want to disappoint their peers or leadership. While this dedication is admirable, it can eventually lead to feelings of resentment and exhaustion when their consistent efforts are met with more work rather than recognition or relief. Leaders must take a more strategic approach, ensuring that workloads are distributed fairly. By protecting the well-being of top performers, agencies not only preserve their leadership potential but also demonstrate a genuine commitment to fairness and sustainability.

Burnout is not solely a product of excessive workload; it is deeply tied to the emotional weight that officers carry. Every shift exposes them to human suffering, violence, and tragedy, experiences that can chip away at their emotional reserves. Over time, this exposure often leads to emotional exhaustion, detachment, and, in severe cases, post-traumatic stress disorder (PTSD). These challenges aren't just hypothetical; they are real and devastating. My agency was profoundly shaken when one of our deputies, Justin, took his own life. Losing him was a tragic wake-up call that underscored the immense toll this career can take on those who serve.

The loss of Justin forced us to confront the uncomfortable truth that law enforcement agencies must do more to address the mental and emotional health of their officers. Wellness initiatives cannot be optional or surface-level; they must be integrated into the fabric of an agency's culture. This includes providing regular access to trauma-focused therapy and offering peer support programs where officers can speak openly with colleagues who understand the unique challenges of the job. When these resources are readily available, officers are better equipped to process their experiences and maintain their resilience.

Debriefing sessions after critical incidents are another essential tool in addressing the emotional toll of the job. These sessions create an environment for officers to unpack their experiences, share their feelings, and seek guidance without fear of judgment. Agencies should normalize these practices, ensuring they are not perceived as remedial measures but as routine, proactive steps in maintaining emotional well-being. A single debriefing session can provide immense relief and prevent long-term emotional damage.

Beyond providing resources, leadership must actively promote a culture of support and understanding. When agency leaders openly acknowledge the emotional challenges of law enforcement, they send a powerful message to their officers: "We see you, we value you, and we are here to help." This sense of support can be a lifeline for officers navigating the dark and difficult moments of their careers.

Preventing tragedies like Justin's requires a multifaceted approach. Agencies need to invest in early intervention strategies to recognize when an officer may be struggling. Training supervisors to identify signs of distress and to empower them to act is crucial. Leadership must also foster an environment where seeking help is seen as a strength, not a weakness, and where officers feel secure in accessing the resources they need.

It's important to remember that supporting officer wellness isn't just about retaining a healthy workforce; it's about preserving lives. Officers who are emotionally healthy are better equipped to serve their communities effectively and safely. By addressing the root causes of burnout and emotional fatigue, agencies can create a culture where officers feel valued and supported. Not just as employees but as people.

The loss of one officer to burnout, emotional exhaustion, or worse, is one too many. Agencies must take deliberate steps to prevent these outcomes by prioritizing wellness, fostering a culture of understanding, and ensuring that no officer feels alone in their struggles. In doing so, they not only honor the memory of those like Justin but also create a foundation for a stronger, healthier future for all who serve.

Promoting work-life balance is a critical but often overlooked component of combating burnout. Law enforcement officers need time to recharge and reconnect with their personal lives. Agencies should consider implementing flexible scheduling, ensuring adequate time off, and creating policies that encourage officers to prioritize their physical and emotional well-being. By recognizing that officers are people with lives outside of the badge, agencies send a strong message that their health and happiness matter.

Leverage data from calls for service, employee surveys, and other relevant metrics to design a schedule that maximizes operational efficiency while prioritizing employee well-being. For example, my agency has seen remarkable success with 12-hour shifts, which offer excellent coverage and provide deputies with approximately 15 days off each month, a significant boost to work-life balance. However, every agency has unique resources and operational needs, so it's essential to tailor your scheduling approach accordingly. Most importantly, employees should be actively involved in the decision-making process whenever possible. When staff feel heard and satisfied with their schedules, they are more likely to remain committed to the agency and less likely to seek opportunities elsewhere.

Addressing burnout and fostering work-life balance is an ethical obligation and strategic necessity for law enforcement agencies. In an increasingly competitive hiring landscape, agencies that prioritize the holistic well-being of their officers stand out as employers of choice. When officers feel supported, valued, and equipped to meet the demands of their profession, they are more likely to remain engaged, motivated, and committed to their roles.

## RECOGNIZING AND VALUING OFFICERS

Recognition is one of the most powerful yet underutilized tools in retaining officers. When individuals feel their efforts are acknowledged and appreciated, they develop a stronger sense of loyalty and commitment to their department. Recognition doesn't always have to be elaborate or formal; sometimes, the smallest gestures, a simple thank-you, a note of appreciation, or an acknowledgment during roll call, can make a world of difference. These moments of recognition remind officers that their hard work is noticed and valued, even in the daily grind of a demanding profession.

However, a culture of recognition goes beyond occasional gratitude. Agencies should establish consistent and structured programs to celebrate their officers' achievements. This can include formal commendations for exceptional performance, milestone awards for years of service, or even monthly recognition for officers who go above and beyond in their duties. Creating a predictable framework for acknowledging accomplishments ensures that recognition becomes an integral part of the department's culture rather than an afterthought.

Publicly celebrating officers' contributions amplifies the impact of recognition. For example, holding a community awards ceremony or publishing a spotlight feature in a department newsletter can highlight the incredible work officers do every day. Public recognition not only boosts individual morale but also fosters pride within the entire department while reinforcing the department's values to the community it serves. It sends a clear message: the agency values and supports its officers.

Peer-to-peer recognition is a powerful tool for fostering a supportive and cohesive work environment. Programs that empower officers to nominate their colleagues for awards or acknowledgment encourage camaraderie, mutual respect, and teamwork. When officers take the time to recognize each other's contributions, it reinforces a sense of shared purpose and strengthens relationships across the department. This kind of recognition is especially meaningful because it comes from those who truly understand the challenges and nuances of the job.

At my agency, we partnered with the Loudoun County Board of Supervisors to establish the Employee Achievements & Contributions to Loudoun County (EMPACT) Awards, a program designed to highlight and reward outstanding performance. What made this program unique was that officers could be nominated not only by agency leadership and supervisors but also by their coworkers. Sometimes, receiving recognition from your coworkers can be even more powerful and meaningful than receiving it from a supervisor. This peer-driven approach fostered a culture where excellence was celebrated at all levels.

The EMPACT Awards program featured four tiers of recognition: bronze, silver, gold, and platinum. Each level came with a monetary award and a formal letter placed in the recipient's employee file, providing both immediate and lasting acknowledgment of their achievements. The platinum award, the highest distinction, was particularly special. It included an annual ceremony where recipients were publicly celebrated for their incredible contributions. This event honored individual officers and served as a morale booster for the entire department, showcasing the value of hard work and dedication.

Programs like EMPACT exemplify how structured and meaningful recognition can elevate an agency's culture. By offering multiple levels of awards and opportunities for peer nominations, agencies can create an environment where every officer feels their contributions matter. This approach not only strengthens bonds within the department but also reinforces a collective commitment to excellence, ensuring that recognition becomes a cornerstone of retention and morale-building efforts.

Ultimately, recognizing and valuing officers is about building a culture of respect and appreciation. When leaders consistently acknowledge their teams' contributions, they create an environment where officers feel seen, supported, and motivated to stay. By prioritizing recognition as a core element of their retention strategy, agencies can strengthen both individual morale and overall departmental cohesion, ensuring their officers remain engaged and dedicated for years to come.

## SUPPORTING MID-CAREER OFFICERS

While agencies should strive to ensure that every member of their department feels valued and supported, it is especially critical to focus retention efforts on mid-career officers. These individuals, often with 5-12 years of experience, occupy a unique and pivotal position within a department. They are no longer rookies needing constant guidance, nor are they seasoned veterans nearing retirement. Instead, they are the backbone of the agency. They are experienced, reliable, and full of potential. Yet, despite their importance, this group is leaving the profession at alarming rates, often citing frustration, lack of career development, and a sense of stagnation.

At this stage in their careers, officers should be on the path to becoming the future leaders of the organization. Many have developed advanced skills, specialized in particular areas, or taken on supervisory responsibilities. However, a recurring theme I encounter through my work with Recruiting Heroes is that many mid-career officers feel stuck. They believe their growth within the agency has plateaued, and they begin to look for opportunities outside law enforcement where their experience and skills are valued.

One key factor driving this exodus is the absence of clear career development opportunities. Mid-career officers often feel they are overlooked for promotions or advanced roles, with no defined path to reach their professional goals. Agencies can address this by implementing structured career development programs that outline specific steps officers can take to advance within the organization. These programs should include mentorship opportunities, cross-training in specialized units, and clearly defined criteria for promotions. Motivated officers must know that they have long-term opportunities with their organization in order to stay fully motivated and engaged. Offering these officers tangible growth opportunities shows them that their future with the agency is valued.

Leadership training is another critical component of retaining mid-career officers. Many in this group aspire to supervisory or command staff roles but feel unprepared or unsupported in pursuing them. By offering leadership classes, workshops, and certifications tailored to law enforcement, agencies can equip these officers with the skills and confidence needed to take on greater responsibilities. Leadership programs also signal that the agency is invested in its long-term success, fostering loyalty and commitment. For example, providing access to courses and programs like the FBI-LEEDA Trilogy, IACP Leadership in Police Organizations, Executive Management Program at the Northwestern Center for Public Safety, and many others can prepare mid-career officers for leadership while reigniting their passion for the profession. It is not enough to have these opportunities buried deep inside employee handbooks or training resources. Agencies should seek out and encourage their mid-career officers and provide them with the time and resources to pursue these opportunities.

Departments must also involve mid-career officers in decision-making processes to make them feel valued and included. Too often, these officers feel their insights and experience are overlooked when policies or initiatives are developed. By creating committees or task forces where mid-career officers can contribute ideas, agencies can tap into a wealth of knowledge and creativity. Whether it's developing new training protocols, updating equipment standards, or improving community engagement strategies, these officers bring a practical, field-tested perspective that can lead to more effective solutions. Moreover, involving them in decisions fosters a sense of ownership and purpose, reinforcing their commitment to the agency.

Recognition remains a cornerstone of retention, particularly for mid-career officers. While new recruits may receive accolades for their enthusiasm and veterans are honored for their years of service, mid-career officers often fall into a recognition gap. Agencies must establish programs that specifically highlight the contributions of this group. For instance, acknowledging their role in mentoring younger officers, managing complex cases, or leading community initiatives can boost morale. Recognition doesn't have to be some elaborate and official event. Sometimes, a heartfelt thank-you or acknowledgment during a department meeting is enough to make these officers feel seen and appreciated.

Proactively addressing burnout among mid-career officers is essential. This group often takes on significant workloads because they are trusted to handle high-stress situations with competence. However, leadership must be cautious not to overburden these individuals. Consistently assigning additional tasks to top performers because they "always get the job done" can lead to resentment and fatigue. Instead, leaders should ensure workloads are distributed equitably and provide opportunities for mid-career officers to recharge, such as sabbaticals, team rotations, or mental health days.

Lastly, fostering a culture of mentorship and succession planning can solidify the role of mid-career officers as integral members of the agency's future. Pairing these officers with senior leaders or assigning them as mentors to newer recruits allows them to see their influence on the department's trajectory. Additionally, involving them in succession planning discussions signals that the agency views them as key players in its long-term success. These initiatives not only benefit the department but also give mid-career officers a renewed sense of purpose and belonging.

By focusing on career development opportunities, leadership training, inclusive decision-making, and proactive support, agencies can retain their mid-career officers and empower them to become the next generation of law enforcement leaders. These efforts will not only reduce attrition but also ensure that agencies maintain a strong, experienced, and motivated workforce capable of navigating the complexities of modern policing.

## BUILDING A RETENTION-FIRST CULTURE

Retention is not the responsibility of one individual or even a single unit. It's a collective effort that requires the engagement of the entire organization. Agencies that excel in retention make it an integral part of their culture, woven into every interaction, policy, and practice. This type of environment starts with leadership but must extend throughout the department. When everyone, from the chief to the newest recruit, is invested in creating a supportive and inspiring workplace, the impact can be transformative.

To build this culture, agencies must focus on collaboration, transparency, and adaptability. Retention-first organizations embrace feedback and challenge outdated practices that no longer serve their purpose. They recognize that every officer brings unique value to the team and ensure that contributions are acknowledged. Instead of viewing officers as interchangeable parts, these agencies treat them as the lifeblood of the department.

Creating an environment that fosters retention involves looking at the entire officer experience. Agencies need to prioritize work-life balance, career growth, and recognition. Flexible schedules, professional development opportunities, and a commitment to wellness all significantly keep officers engaged and committed. Retention isn't just about offering perks. It's about building trust, demonstrating genuine care, and fostering a sense of belonging.

Leadership plays a pivotal role in this process. Supervisors and command staff must model behaviors that show officers they are valued. This means acknowledging hard work, advocating for necessary resources, and providing opportunities for growth. When leaders actively demonstrate their commitment to the well-being and development of their team, it sets the tone for the entire department and inspires officers to do the same in their interactions with colleagues and the community.

One of the most effective ways to build a retention-first culture is to involve officers in decision-making processes. Agencies that give their employees a voice, whether through advisory committees, focus groups, or regular one-on-one check-ins, show that they value their input. When officers feel heard and empowered, they become more invested in the success of the organization. This sense of ownership can also lead to innovative ideas and solutions that benefit the entire agency.

Mentorship programs are another powerful tool for retention. Pairing experienced officers with newer recruits creates opportunities for knowledge-sharing and builds strong support networks. These relationships can help prevent burnout by providing guidance and encouragement during challenging times. Similarly, peer support programs offer a space for officers to discuss difficulties and work through them collaboratively, fostering camaraderie and mutual trust.

Career development opportunities are essential for keeping officers engaged and motivated. Agencies that invest in leadership classes, specialized training, and certifications send a clear message that they are committed to their officers' long-term success. Whether it's hosting workshops on conflict resolution or providing tuition reimbursement for advanced education, these efforts not only equip officers with valuable skills but also reignite their passion for the profession.

Recognition is equally important. A culture that celebrates successes, both big and small, goes a long way in boosting morale. From informal thank-yous to formal awards ceremonies, acknowledging hard work reinforces positive behavior and shows officers their efforts are appreciated. Publicly celebrating milestones, such as anniversaries or promotions, inspires others and strengthens the overall sense of community within the agency.

Providing opportunities for lateral growth is another effective strategy. Not every officer aspires to climb the ranks, but many are eager to expand their skills and take on new challenges. Cross-training in different units or participating in specialized task forces can keep officers engaged and excited about their work. These experiences also diversify their skill sets, making them even more valuable to the agency.

Retention strategies must also adapt to the needs of a multigenerational workforce. Younger officers often value mentorship, work-life balance, and technological integration, while more seasoned officers may prioritize job stability and leadership opportunities. Tailoring approaches to meet these varied needs ensures that all employees feel supported and understood, regardless of where they are in their careers.

Ultimately, retention is not just a strategy. It's a necessity. Agencies that fail to prioritize their officers' well-being and professional growth will face high turnover rates, low morale, and diminished public trust. On the other hand, agencies that invest in their people will retain their best officers and attract top talent who want to be part of a thriving, supportive team. The future of law enforcement depends on whether agencies are willing to take the steps needed to create sustainable, committed workforces. Building a retention-first culture is not easy, but the rewards for the agency, its officers, and the community it serves are well worth the effort. The recruiting strategies we will discuss throughout this book will be of little benefit to your agency if you have not already built a culture of comradery, trust, and retention.

# CHAPTER THREE
# THE MODERN DAY OFFICER

Law enforcement agencies must first take a step back and clearly identify their ideal candidate to address today's recruitment challenges effectively. Recruitment isn't just about filling positions—it's about finding individuals who can meet the demands of a rapidly evolving profession. In today's complex and ever-changing landscape, law enforcement agencies cannot rely solely on traditional hiring models that focus on filling positions with the next available candidate. Instead, they must consider what qualities, skills, and values make up their ideal recruit to ensure they attract officers who align with the department's mission and the evolving expectations of the community. This targeted approach helps ensure new hires meet the department's specific needs and improves long-term retention by bringing in individuals committed to the agency's goals. Only by thoroughly defining and understanding your department's ideal candidate can your team develop and implement a successful recruiting strategy that can target and attract those ideal candidates.

Identifying your department's perfect candidate starts with analyzing the demands and priorities of the agency and the community it serves. Law enforcement officers today need more than just physical and technical skills; they need to embody emotional intelligence, empathy, cultural competence, and the ability to adapt to the dynamic needs of the public. Agencies must assess the traits most essential for officers working within their jurisdiction. For example, officers

COLIN WHITTINGTON

in urban areas may need stronger community engagement skills to build trust in diverse neighborhoods, while rural agencies might prioritize candidates with self-sufficiency and resourcefulness.

A clear understanding of the ideal candidate allows agencies to craft recruitment messages that resonate more effectively with target applicants. Facing an unprecedented number of vacancies, many agencies adopt recruitment strategies aimed simply at filling as many of their positions as quickly as possible, often without fully considering the specific qualities they hope to attract. While hiring candidates from diverse backgrounds is crucial to the future of law enforcement, recruitment efforts that lack a well-defined focus can lead to diluted outcomes, reducing the overall effectiveness of hiring strategies.

By clearly defining the desired attributes and values, agencies can create messaging that appeals directly to candidates who share those qualities. For example, suppose an agency seeks officers with a strong commitment to social responsibility and community service. In that case, it can highlight how the role enables them to make meaningful contributions to society, ensuring public safety and promoting justice. The department can highlight its Community Policing Unit, post pictures of officers showing off their cruisers to children, or share stories of community events they have attended. This targeted recruitment approach is more likely to attract individuals motivated by the opportunity to make a positive impact in society.

Now more than ever, agencies must adopt a strategic and targeted approach to recruitment, beginning with a deep understanding of the qualities, skills, and values essential for success in modern law enforcement. This involves moving away from a one-size-fits-all approach and focusing on the specific attributes that will help recruits thrive in today's environment. Key competencies include technological proficiency, cultural competence, and commitment to community engagement. Today's recruits are often digital natives, accustomed to rapid technological change and high levels of connectivity. As such, they expect law enforcement agencies to embrace technological advancements and offer roles that incorporate modern tools and practices. Agencies must clearly define what they seek in a candidate and tailor their recruitment efforts accordingly. A well-defined profile of the ideal candidate will guide these efforts, ensuring that recruitment strategies are both focused and effective.

In the competitive landscape of law enforcement recruitment, clearly defining the ideal candidate provides agencies with a critical advantage. It not only allows departments to stand out by promoting the values, culture, and opportunities that will attract the right individuals, but it also ensures that those who join the agency are well-suited for the challenges of modern policing. By focusing on this alignment between agency needs and the desired characteristics of their ideal recruits, law enforcement departments can enhance the effectiveness of their recruitment efforts and the overall quality of their workforce.

## A NEW GENERATION

As law enforcement agencies navigate the evolving recruitment landscape, it's imperative that agencies recognize the generational shifts at play, particularly concerning Millennials and Generation Z. Historically, law enforcement, similarly to the military, has relied heavily on recruiting young candidates to join the ranks. While agencies receive the occasional application from a candidate in their 40s or 50s, the majority of candidates interested in joining the law enforcement profession are in their 20s and early 30s. Currently, that means agencies heavily rely on attracting candidates from the Millennial and Generation Z generations.

To successfully recruit the new generation of law enforcement officers, it is critical to understand their unique values and motivations. The dynamics of law enforcement recruitment are evolving rapidly, driven by the distinct values, motivations, and expectations of the Millennials and Generation Z. These younger generations bring a fresh perspective to the workforce, prioritizing purpose, social justice, flexibility, growth opportunities, and work-life balance. They are drawn to careers that not only provide stability but also align with their values and allow them to make a meaningful impact in the world around them. Law enforcement agencies that fail to reflect these values in their messaging and opportunities will struggle to capture the interest of these individuals. To successfully recruit and retain talent from these cohorts, law enforcement agencies must deeply understand the generational differences between the candidates who entered the profession in the 20th and early 21st centuries and those who may look to become law enforcement officers today.

Traditionally, law enforcement agencies have attracted individuals from older generations who were motivated by a sense of duty, job security, and long-term benefits such as pensions. Baby Boomer and Gen X officers were accustomed to rigid structures, hierarchical leadership, a live-to-work mentality, and the expectation that they would remain with an organization for decades. Many accepted long hours and the inherent risk of the job without seeking much beyond a steady paycheck and a strong retirement plan.

Millennials (those born between 1981 and 1996) and Generation Z (those born after 1996), however, view their careers entirely differently from their parents. While previous generations valued having a stable job, today's youth prioritize meaningful work, personal growth, work-life balance, and a supportive and inclusive work environment. The rise of technology has increased job mobility, and a changing global landscape has reshaped their expectations for their employers. Understanding these shifts in mindsets is critical for law enforcement agencies aiming to attract and retain younger officers.

To effectively recruit Millennials and Gen Z candidates, departments must understand the core drivers that attract these groups to a career. A key factor in attracting Millennials and Generation Z candidates is demonstrating that law enforcement offers more than just a job; it must be portrayed as a career that provides both personal fulfillment and opportunities for advancement. These generations are drawn to work that feels meaningful, where they can make a real difference. So many agencies try to attract candidates by simply advertising top-end salaries or huge hiring bonuses. However, those aren't always the biggest concerns for young candidates driven to make a difference in the world. By highlighting how law enforcement careers allow individuals to contribute to their communities and society, agencies can appeal to their desire for purpose-driven work.

Millennials and Generation Z are deeply committed to social change and want their work to reflect their values. To attract these candidates, law enforcement agencies should highlight officers' critical role in addressing community safety, equality, and social justice. By framing the profession as an opportunity to positively impact these areas, agencies can appeal to candidates driven by a desire to create a safer and happier society.

Social media can be a powerful tool in this effort. While we'll explore its role in recruitment later in the book, it's essential that your agency's social media consistently showcases officers engaging with the community, making a difference, and building trust. Although not every post needs an explicit recruiting angle, regularly demonstrating your agency's commitment to social initiatives will strengthen your recruiting efforts and resonate with candidates who value meaningful, impactful work.

Additionally, emphasizing the role of law enforcement officers as agents of positive change can help reshape perceptions of the profession. By showcasing how officers can contribute to building community trust and promoting justice, agencies can appeal to individuals passionate about making a meaningful impact. This approach aligns with the values of younger generations and positions law enforcement as a career path with significant societal influence.

Work-life balance is a top priority for many Millennials and Generation Z candidates, and law enforcement agencies must acknowledge this when recruiting. Unlike previous generations, the new workforce emphasizes maintaining a healthy equilibrium between their professional and personal lives. Therefore, agencies must demonstrate that they respect their officers' personal time and are committed to creating a supportive work environment that fosters this balance.

Agencies can address work-life balance concerns by offering flexible work schedules that allow officers to manage their time effectively while accommodating personal and family needs. During my time overseeing our agency's recruiting unit, we strongly promoted and advertised our 12-hour shift schedule, which provides officers with 15 days off each month. This was a significant selling point for many candidates. Additionally, our agency implemented a "shift bid" system, allowing officers to request shift changes every six months. While these bids weren't guaranteed, officers who consistently requested a shift change were often accommodated more quickly than at other law enforcement agencies. This level of flexibility, both in shift scheduling and accommodating preferences, reassures candidates that they won't be stuck on undesired shifts for years. By prioritizing these efforts, agencies can demonstrate their commitment to officers' personal lives, making law enforcement a more appealing career choice for those who value balance.

Wellness programs are a critical aspect that law enforcement agencies should highlight in their recruitment efforts. Programs focusing on physical fitness, mental health resources, and stress management demonstrate that the agency values the overall well-being of its officers. In today's job market, younger candidates are especially drawn to workplaces that prioritize health and wellness. By showcasing comprehensive wellness programs, agencies can appeal to Millennials and Generation Z, who increasingly understand the importance of maintaining physical and mental health.

For instance, at the Loudoun County Sheriff's Office, deputies can work out for one hour per shift, provided calls for service allow it. This policy not only supports the physical health of deputies but also acknowledges the need for a healthy work-life balance. What makes this program particularly effective is the agency's encouragement for deputies to take advantage of this hour without fear of being looked down upon for doing so. A policy that allows physical exercise during work is of very little benefit if participants are punished or criticized for using it. Highlighting this initiative was hugely successful in our efforts to attract candidates who value fitness and see law enforcement as a career that respects their well-being.

In addition to physical wellness, mental health support must be emphasized as a key benefit of the profession. Younger generations are looking for assurance that their mental health will be prioritized, given the stressful nature of law enforcement. Consider implementing a peer support system where deputies and officers can contact colleagues trained to provide emotional and psychological assistance. This type of program offers an invaluable resource for officers, allowing them to manage the stress and trauma they may encounter on the job without fear of retribution. Some departments have taken it a step further by funding full-time psychologist positions to ensure the mental well-being of those who often see the worst parts of humanity. Agencies offering these types of mental health support systems will stand out to younger candidates who value a healthy work environment and their well-being.

Departments that offer additional mental health programs to ensure the overall wellness of their officers should highlight these initiatives as part of their recruiting efforts. By creating an environment where seeking mental health support is encouraged and accessible, agencies foster a culture of well-being that appeals to candidates who are mindful of mental health in their professional lives while also ensuring the overall health and wellness of their officers, leading to a stronger workforce and better retention rates.

Agencies that prioritize and promote physical fitness, mental health, and overall wellness create a compelling case for younger recruits. With Millennials and Generation Z placing high importance on work environments supporting their well-being, these programs become a key factor in recruitment efforts. By demonstrating a commitment to officer wellness, law enforcement agencies can attract candidates looking for a career that not only challenges them but also supports their long-term health and happiness while drastically improving the retention and overall satisfaction of their current staff.

To effectively attract Millennials and Generation Z to law enforcement careers, agencies must go beyond traditional recruiting messages and emphasize the promise of continuous learning and meaningful career development. Younger candidates are driven by opportunities to grow personally and professionally, seeking careers that challenge them, equip them with valuable skills, and offer clear paths for advancement. Agencies should actively showcase the diverse training programs, certifications, and specialized skill-building opportunities available to officers throughout their careers. For example, if your agency offers advanced training such as Explosive Ordnance Disposal (EOD), crisis negotiation, or specialized tactical courses, these should take center stage in your recruiting materials. Similarly, prestigious leadership programs like FBI-LEEDA or opportunities to earn advanced degrees can serve as powerful incentives for candidates prioritizing growth and career development.

Educational and professional development opportunities should be integrated into the description of what distinguishes a career in law enforcement. Recruits need to see that law enforcement is not a static occupation confined to routine tasks but a dynamic and evolving career path with limitless potential for those willing to invest in themselves. Highlighting these opportunities not only positions law enforcement as a forward-thinking profession but also helps dispel outdated stereotypes of police work as rigid or unchanging.

To truly resonate with these younger generations, agencies should frame these opportunities in ways that align with their values and interests. For instance, showcase how training programs can build transferable skills, such as crisis management, leadership, or advanced technology proficiency, which are valuable in and beyond law enforcement. Agencies can also emphasize mentorship programs, career specialization tracks, and internal pathways to promotion, illustrating that the agency is committed to nurturing talent and helping officers reach their full potential.

Additionally, consider leveraging current officers as ambassadors to share their stories. A detective who began their career in patrol and later transitioned into cybercrime investigations or an officer who took part in international training initiatives can offer compelling, relatable examples of the growth potential within the profession. Pair these testimonials with visuals of officers engaged in training exercises or leadership seminars to create a vivid, inspiring portrayal of a law enforcement career as an ongoing journey of learning, achievement, and impact.

Agencies can enhance their appeal and attract motivated, ambitious candidates, particularly from Millennial and Generation Z demographics, by showcasing the diverse career paths within law enforcement. From community policing and victim advocacy to cybercrime investigation, the profession offers meaningful opportunities catering to various interests and skill sets. By emphasizing this diversity and signaling a commitment to supporting officers' long-term success, agencies can enrich their workforce and strengthen the perception of law enforcement as a progressive, impactful, and rewarding career choice.

Millennials and Generation Z have come of age in a world defined by rapid technological advancement, shaping their expectations for innovation and efficiency in the workplace. These digital natives embrace modern tools and view their integration as essential to productivity, communication, and overall job satisfaction. To resonate with this mindset, law enforcement agencies must actively position themselves as forward-thinking organizations that leverage cutting-edge technology to enhance operations and effectiveness. Simply put, younger generations want to see that policing is evolving alongside the rest of the world and are eager to be part of that evolution.

Agencies that adopt advanced technologies such as body-worn cameras, real-time data analytics, and mobile platforms for field operations will naturally appeal to tech-savvy candidates. These tools also demonstrate a commitment to transparency, accountability, and

COLIN WHITTINGTON

efficiency, values that deeply resonate with younger generations. Highlighting the agency's use of innovative systems like drones for aerial surveillance, License Plate Readers (LPRs) for intelligence gathering, or automated systems for administrative tasks can also spark interest among candidates who are drawn to roles where they can interact with cutting-edge equipment and contribute to more innovative policing strategies.

However, it's not enough to simply implement these tools; agencies must actively showcase their use in recruitment efforts. Including visuals or videos of officers utilizing drones to monitor large-scale events, leveraging advanced forensic technologies, or operating state-of-the-art crime mapping software can captivate potential recruits and illustrate how modern policing integrates innovation into everyday responsibilities. Testimonials from current officers who have embraced these technologies can further reinforce the agency's tech-forward approach, offering first-hand accounts of how such tools have transformed their work and improved public safety outcomes.

Incorporating a focus on technology into recruitment materials signals to Millennials and Gen Z that the agency not only understands their priorities but is also committed to staying ahead of the curve in the ever-changing landscape of modern law enforcement. It paints a compelling picture of a career that is as innovative as it is impactful, where recruits can contribute to meaningful change while being equipped with the tools to succeed. By embracing and promoting technological advancements, agencies can position themselves as employers of choice for the next generation of law enforcement professionals.

Understanding and defining the ideal recruit allows law enforcement agencies to craft compelling and focused recruitment strategies. This targeted approach helps attract candidates who are not only interested in law enforcement but also well-suited for its evolving challenges. By refining recruitment goals and strategies, agencies can build a more capable and committed workforce, ultimately reducing turnover and enhancing overall effectiveness. This focused approach also allows agencies to allocate recruitment resources strategically, ensuring efforts are concentrated where they will be most effective.

In a world where the competition to attract talent is fiercer than ever, law enforcement agencies that are committed to understanding and adapting to the values of Millennials and Generation Z are the ones that will stand out above the rest. These generations seek purposeful, supportive, and progressive workplaces that value their contributions, support their well-being, and offer career growth opportunities. By aligning recruitment efforts with these core values and emphasizing areas like wellness, community impact, career development, and technology, agencies can foster a workforce that is both effective and committed to the long-term goals of public safety and community engagement

Ultimately, attracting and retaining the next generation of officers will require more than traditional hiring approaches. It demands a proactive, tailored strategy that reflects an agency's willingness to adapt to the evolving priorities of today's recruits. Agencies that make these adjustments demonstrate an investment not only in their future officers but also in the community's trust and the profession's reputation. With this comprehensive approach, law enforcement agencies can better navigate the complex recruitment landscape, ensuring that they bring on board officers who are dedicated, resilient, and ready to positively impact their communities.

# CHAPTER FOUR
# THROW OUT THE HANDBOOK

Spend some time in the profession, and you'll quickly learn that law enforcement has historically been slow to change, with agencies often clinging to long-established practices and traditions even as society evolves. As societal norms, technologies, and public expectations have rapidly advanced, law enforcement agencies frequently lag behind. My agency, for example, still issued their new deputies pagers and flip phones all the way until 2018, with most new hires having never used a pager in their entire lives and having become so accustomed to utilizing smartphones that reverting to an almost forgotten technology took some adjusting. Many law enforcement departments were slow to implement Crisis Intervention Training, officer wellness initiatives, and other critical programs despite years of pressure from staff and members of the public. These are just some of the countless examples of law enforcement often being behind the rest of society in adjusting their policies, procedures, and equipment.

This reluctance to evolve has created significant challenges in addressing modern-day issues, particularly in areas like recruitment and retention. As the profession has been slow to adapt, it faces mounting difficulties in attracting and retaining talent, especially from a new generation that values technological integration and progressive workplace practices. The gap between traditional methods and modern expectations has become increasingly apparent, making it clear that outdated approaches are inadequate for meeting the needs of today's diverse and tech-savvy candidates.

Many current law enforcement agencies are still led by a generation of officers who began their careers in an era vastly different from the one facing today's recruits. Leaders from this period recall times when hundreds of candidates would eagerly line up for the agency's monthly candidate testing dates, with only a handful of police officer positions available. A simple newspaper advertisement could yield a flood of applicants, and it was common for departments to be fully staffed, a stark contrast to the chronic staffing shortages many agencies face today. This historical abundance of candidates underscores the dramatic shift in the recruitment landscape over the years. It creates mental barriers for law enforcement executives unfamiliar with the current recruitment and retention challenges or the drastic measures necessary to address them.

For law enforcement executives from this older generation, coming to terms with the modern recruitment and retention challenges can be particularly difficult. The gap between the past and present is not just a matter of nostalgia but reflects a fundamental shift in societal values, technological advancements, and job market dynamics. Executives accustomed to a more straightforward recruitment process may struggle to adapt to today's complex environment, where attracting and retaining talent requires innovative strategies, consistent efforts, additional funding, and a deep understanding of present-day candidates' expectations. Addressing these challenges requires a willingness to embrace change and an openness to new approaches that align with the needs and preferences of today's workforce.

## TRADITIONAL VS. MODERN RECRUITMENT

For decades, law enforcement agencies have relied heavily on traditional recruiting methods such as walk-ins, local advertisements, career fairs, and word of mouth to meet their hiring needs. These strategies were effective throughout the late 20th and early 21st centuries, providing a consistent flow of candidates to fill the limited vacancies in police departments and sheriff's offices nationwide. These methods aligned well with the expectations and habits of the Baby Boomers and Generation X, the primary candidates entering the law enforcement profession. Print media, television advertisements, and community outreach programs were effective tools that attracted a steady stream of applicants eager to serve their communities.

However, as the demographic landscape shifts, these traditional methods are proving increasingly inadequate. The recruiting tactics that once resonated with Baby Boomers and Generation X are now falling flat with Millennials and Generation Z, who are more digitally connected and diverse. These younger generations grew up in a world where information is consumed through screens rather than print and where social media and online platforms play a central role in daily life. The decline in the effectiveness of traditional recruiting methods can be attributed to this shift in how younger generations engage with the world around them.

Today's younger candidates, many of whom have never even picked up a physical newspaper, are unlikely to be reached through outdated advertising channels. Yet, despite the clear evidence that these methods are no longer effective, some police departments continue to rely on local print ads, radio marketing, and evening news broadcasts to fill their ranks. Others simply upload their police officer job opening on their local government's website, hoping candidates will find it and apply. This reliance on outdated recruiting methods represents a significantly missed opportunity to connect with a new generation of potential officers who are more likely to be found on digital platforms than in the pages of a newspaper or watching the nightly news. Furthermore, the passive form of recruiting utilized by so many agencies will continue to prove ineffective in connecting with candidates who have come to expect a more personalized and proactive recruiting approach from potential employers.

During my time in my agency's Employment Services Section, I often briefed senior command staff members on our recruiting efforts. These law enforcement executives frequently suggested that we advertise in local newspapers, on the evening news, or through other outdated methods, convinced that these were prime channels to reach our ideal candidates. While these methods were effective in the past, I had to explain that not only would these options be prohibitively expensive, but they would also be ineffective in attracting anyone under the age of 40 or 50 to join the sheriff's office. Like the military, law enforcement relies on a steady stream of young candidates to fill their ranks. By utilizing recruiting methods that fail to reach the younger demographic, law enforcement agencies are all but ensuring an ongoing vacancy crisis.

How many people under the age of 40 do you know who still use cable? Among my friends, I was one of the few who did until the end of last year, when I also gave up. Of the small percentage of Millennials and Gen Z who have cable, almost none of them get their news from traditional sources, preferring to learn about current events through social media. Streaming services, on-demand content, and social media platforms have largely replaced traditional television viewing among younger generations. As a result, advertising on television, particularly during the evening news, is unlikely to reach most of the target demographic that law enforcement agencies are trying to recruit.

Now, think about newspapers and other forms of print media. How many 20- or 30-year-olds still read them? Most have probably never even picked up a physical newspaper before. The decline of print media has been well-documented, with readership steadily decreasing as more people turn to digital sources for their news and information. This shift has rendered local print ads, once a staple of law enforcement recruitment, increasingly ineffective in reaching potential recruits.

One of the biggest mistakes I see law enforcement agencies make is relying on local government websites as the sole platform for posting job openings. In the private sector, companies use applicant tracking systems to broadcast their open positions on dozens of job boards simultaneously, reaching a broad and diverse pool of potential candidates. In contrast, most law enforcement agencies stick to their own outdated websites or, even worse, bury their job openings on their city's or county government's websites. This means candidates would need to proactively seek out these openings rather than come across them through everyday job searching. By failing to post their positions on more popular job platforms, these agencies severely limit their applicant pool, missing out on numerous qualified candidates who could stumble upon the job by chance. The rigid, localized approach ignores the fact that the modern job market requires a more proactive and far-reaching recruitment strategy.

The absence of law enforcement job listings on major platforms like LinkedIn, Indeed, ZipRecruiter, and Monster is a glaring oversight. These platforms are crucial tools for recruitment, providing access to millions of active job seekers across various industries and demographics. LinkedIn alone boasts over 900 million users globally, yet most law enforcement agencies have failed to adopt it as part of their recruitment efforts. Private sector companies recognize the power of these platforms and use them to their full potential, reaching not just active job seekers but also professionals who may not even be thinking about a career change until the right opportunity is presented to them. By not leveraging these resources, law enforcement agencies are missing out on some of today's most powerful and widely used recruiting tools.

The problem is further compounded by the generally outdated and uninviting nature of many law enforcement websites. When potential candidates seek out law enforcement jobs, they are often met with bland and poorly designed websites offering little information beyond basic job requirements. There is rarely an in-depth explanation of what a career in law enforcement entails, the benefits of joining a particular department, recruiter contact information, or any compelling visuals or testimonials from current officers. This lack of engaging content does nothing to draw in potential recruits. A key part of any successful recruiting strategy is creating a strong first impression. Unfortunately, many agencies fail in this regard.

When I took over my agency's Employment Services Section, one of my first initiatives was creating a standalone recruiting website dedicated to showcasing our department as an attractive workplace. This site was designed to be informative and visually appealing, with sections outlining what it takes to become a deputy sheriff, an overview of our background and hiring process, details on employee benefits, and pictures and testimonials from current staff members. We also included a calendar of recruiting events so interested candidates could engage with us directly. Though it required a lot of time and effort to put together, the cost was minimal compared to the long-term benefits it provided to my former agency's recruitment efforts. The site became a valuable resource, helping us to project a modern, professional image that resonates with today's job seekers.

Every law enforcement agency should strive for a similar approach and create a standalone recruiting website. At the very least, departments should ensure their agency's websites feature a dedicated recruitment and careers page. Simply listing your agency's open positions on your careers page is insufficient. The page should give candidates a sense of what your agency stands for, the benefits of a career in law enforcement, and the steps they'll need to take to join. Providing transparent information about the application and hiring process, the benefits offered, and what makes the department unique is essential to attract quality candidates. Job seekers in today's market expect to be well-informed. Agencies that fail to provide candidates with a comprehensive view of what sets them apart will find themselves at a disadvantage in a highly competitive job market.

In the modern era, the digital landscape is often the first point of contact between agencies and potential recruits, and it's vital that this first impression is a positive one. A well-designed, informative recruitment site can make all the difference in turning a passive job seeker into an active applicant. By embracing modern recruiting tools, creating engaging online content, and utilizing major job platforms, law enforcement agencies can expand their reach, attract a more diverse pool of candidates, and, ultimately, fill their ranks with the best and brightest recruits. To remain competitive, law enforcement agencies must stop relying solely on traditional methods and adopt more innovative strategies that have proven successful in the private sector.

One of the few traditional recruiting methods I believe still holds value in modern-day recruitment strategies is on-site career events or job fairs. These events allow law enforcement agencies to engage with potential recruits face-to-face, creating a unique platform for direct communication. Job fairs allow candidates to ask questions, gain a deeper understanding of the profession, and develop a personal connection with the agency. In-person interactions at these events can be pivotal, as they offer potential recruits the chance to meet officers and recruiters who could become their future colleagues. This personalized approach helps build trust and offers candidates a first-hand perspective of the agency's culture, values, and expectations.

From my experience, attending these events was not only about recruiting new officers but also about networking with other law enforcement agencies. I often found these job fairs to be an excellent learning opportunity where I could exchange ideas and discover what other departments were doing to attract quality applicants. Observing various recruitment strategies allowed my agency to stay competitive and innovate in our own approach to hiring. Additionally, attending these events helped spread awareness of our agency's brand, reinforcing our commitment to community engagement and career development for recruits.

However, on-site career fairs are not without their challenges. These events are time-consuming and often have a significant financial burden for agencies. Signing up for a booth at a career fair is just the first cost; additional expenses include transportation, lodging, per diem for officers, promotional materials, and the salaries of the recruiters attending. Agencies often allocate substantial portions of their recruitment budgets to participate in these events, hoping the investment will yield quality candidates over time. This financial outlay can be particularly challenging for smaller departments with limited resources, leading to difficult decisions about where to allocate funds.

Moreover, the return on investment from these events is not always immediate. Many career fairs, especially at universities, are aimed at college students who may not be ready to apply for a law enforcement position for several months or even years. Agencies may have to wait for these potential candidates to finish their degrees or complete other prerequisites before they can submit applications. This delay in receiving applications can make it difficult to assess the success of a particular event, as the benefits may not become evident for quite some time. For law enforcement leaders accustomed to seeing immediate results from their actions, the long-term timeline of recruiting can be challenging to come to terms with. In a later chapter, we will discuss the importance of tracking metrics and analyzing recruiting data.

Despite the costs and delayed results, on-site career fairs still play a critical role in law enforcement recruitment. They allow agencies to make meaningful connections with potential recruits and provide candidates with a tangible sense of what it means to serve in the profession. While it may be necessary to complement these events with more cost-effective digital recruitment strategies, in-person career fairs remain a valuable tool for engaging the next generation of law enforcement officers.

To address the evolving needs of modern law enforcement recruitment, agencies can make small yet impactful adjustments to traditional recruiting methods. While in-person career fairs remain valuable for fostering personal connections, agencies can enhance these events by integrating technology, such as offering virtual components or live-streaming information sessions. This hybrid approach allows agencies to maintain the benefits of face-to-face interactions while broadening their reach to candidates who cannot attend in person.

Virtual job fairs offer a modern solution that allows agencies to reach a larger pool of potential candidates without the geographical limitations of in-person events. With the help of technology, agencies can host interactive, online recruitment sessions where candidates can ask questions, learn about the department's culture, and even participate in one-on-one interviews. These events can be structured to mimic the personal interactions of traditional job fairs while being far more flexible and cost-effective.

One of the most significant advantages of virtual recruiting events is the substantial cost reduction. Agencies can allocate their recruiting budgets more efficiently without the need for travel, lodging, per diem, or venue expenses. The costs of setting up a virtual platform are typically much lower than those associated with organizing in-person events. Additionally, agencies can save time and resources by allowing recruiters to participate from their own offices or homes, avoiding the logistical challenges of sending personnel to multiple locations. This streamlined approach reduces the financial burden while still providing candidates with an engaging recruitment experience.

Another key benefit of virtual recruiting is the ability to reach candidates from across the country. In contrast to traditional job fairs, which are often limited to a specific region or campus, virtual events allow agencies to cast a wider net and engage with a more diverse group of potential recruits. This expanded reach is especially valuable for law enforcement agencies facing recruitment shortages or looking to attract candidates with specialized skills from outside their immediate area. Connecting with individuals who may not have considered relocating to the agency's jurisdiction opens new avenues for recruitment and diversity within the department. This is particularly powerful for agencies that offer relocation assistance for newly hired officers who join the agencies from other parts of the country.

Furthermore, virtual recruiting events offer candidates greater flexibility, as they can participate from anywhere with an internet con-

COLIN WHITTINGTON

nection. This accessibility makes it easier for individuals who may have busy schedules, are currently employed, or live far away to attend the event without the inconvenience or expense of travel. It also allows agencies to schedule events at different times of day, catering to various time zones and ensuring more people can participate. This convenience enhances the likelihood of engaging with a broader audience of potential recruits who might not have been able to attend an in-person event.

While virtual events may lack the in-person touch of traditional career fairs, they can still provide an interactive and personalized experience for candidates. Agencies can utilize video conferencing, live Q&A sessions, virtual breakout rooms, and even digital tours of the department to create an engaging environment. By integrating multimedia presentations and interactive features, agencies can effectively communicate their values, goals, and opportunities to potential recruits, fostering the same sense of connection and trust that face-to-face interactions provide. When done thoughtfully, virtual recruiting events can serve as a powerful complement to traditional methods, offering agencies a cost-effective and expansive way to connect with the next generation of law enforcement officers. Agencies can better navigate the evolving recruitment landscape by combining on-site career fairs with modern, tech-savvy approaches.

Virtual recruiting events exemplify how law enforcement agencies can and must adapt to modern recruitment techniques that resonate with today's younger, tech-savvy generation. Agencies relying solely on traditional methods risk overlooking a vast pool of candidates who are more accessible through digital marketing and virtual events. As traditional media loses its former influence, agencies must recognize this shift and update their recruitment strategies to stay competitive in an increasingly digital world.

To meet these challenges, law enforcement agencies must fully embrace modern recruitment tactics that appeal to younger candidates. This involves leveraging social media, digital platforms, and data-driven marketing strategies to connect with potential recruits where they are most engaged. Agencies that have adopted these approaches are already seeing the benefits, attracting a more diverse and skilled workforce prepared for the technological demands of modern policing. In the chapters ahead, we will explore further innovative methods to enhance recruitment efforts.

# CHAPTER FIVE
# RECRUITING IN THE DIGITAL AGE

In today's digital age, online platforms have evolved far beyond tools for simple communication and information gathering. They are now essential for shaping public perceptions, engaging communities, and recruiting the next generation of law enforcement professionals. From social media and job boards to professional networking sites, law enforcement agencies have a unique opportunity to leverage a range of digital channels for their recruiting efforts. Each platform offers a cost-effective pathway to connect with potential recruits and the public, allowing agencies to promote transparency, build trust, and attract candidates with the values and skills necessary to serve in this noble profession.

The ability of law enforcement to shape public perception through digital platforms is invaluable. Social media, networking sites such as LinkedIn, and professional websites allow agencies to highlight not only the responsibilities and challenges of policing, but also the dedication to public safety and community service that drives the profession. This outreach is critical in an era where digital impressions often influence public opinion. By providing an authentic view of their work, agencies can dispel misconceptions and present a balanced, humanized image that appeals to a wide range of audiences. Agencies that use social media effectively can highlight their officers' outstanding work, foster public trust, and educate citizens about what a law enforcement career entails.

Job boards and recruitment-focused websites must become vital channels for attracting a new generation of law enforcement professionals. Digital recruitment allows agencies to reach candidates who might not otherwise consider law enforcement as a career path. By using targeted messaging on popular job sites, agencies can craft job descriptions and advertisements that appeal to candidates' desires for meaningful work, career development, and positive community impact. This approach broadens the pool of applicants and attracts individuals whose values align with the agency's mission. However, utilizing the vast potential of social media and digital marketing will require agencies to adjust long-held beliefs and practices.

Networking platforms, particularly those aimed at professional development, also offer opportunities to engage with experienced professionals, potential recruits, and community leaders. Platforms like LinkedIn allow law enforcement agencies to share thought leadership, highlight officer achievements, and engage in industry-wide conversations. Agencies can connect with those who might be considering a career in law enforcement, answer questions, provide mentorship opportunities, and reinforce a culture of professional growth that appeals to a wide range of talent.

In the private sector, companies have become highly proactive in their recruitment methods, leveraging digital tools to find and attract top talent long before candidates even consider applying to that organization. By identifying ideal candidates, companies can take intentional steps to engage with them, ensuring they capture their interest early and often. This strategy goes beyond simply posting job openings and waiting for candidates to apply. It's about proactively and continuously seeking out talent and attracting them to your organization. Do you think the world's largest companies, such as Apple, Microsoft, Google, Amazon, and Walmart, are just waiting for candidates to come to them? No, they are actively seeking out the best talent from around the world to join their organizations. They do this by consistently putting out content that proves their expertise and status in their given industries, drawing the attention and admiration of candidates who are looking to make a career in that field.

The competition for the best candidates is intense, with companies vying to bring talented individuals on board before their competitors can. As a result, recruiters are expected to initiate conversations with promising candidates, even if they are not actively looking for or applying for new opportunities at that time. These "passive" candidates, highly qualified individuals unaware of specific job openings, become the focus, with companies tailoring messages to encourage them to consider the organization. The world's best recruiters can identify these individuals and convince them to join their organization through consistent and proactive recruitment and relationship building.

Addressing the nationwide shortage of law enforcement officers will require agencies to adopt similarly proactive approaches. Many police departments, sheriff's offices, and federal agencies still take a largely reactive stance toward recruitment. This approach is limited to posting job listings on agency websites, attending several career fairs, and occasionally sharing recruitment posts on social media. Once applications come in, they are typically reviewed by staff with little specialized training in recruitment, focusing primarily on discovering any disqualifying factors in their personal history rather than identifying unique attributes that could make a candidate a fantastic choice for a career in law enforcement.

Many law enforcement agencies rely on a reactive recruitment approach that fails to address the critical need to identify and engage talented individuals who aren't actively searching for jobs but would excel as police officers, deputy sheriffs, or federal agents. These "passive" candidates often only need to hear the right message delivered at the right time to consider joining the Thin Blue Line. Unfortunately, few agencies take the necessary steps to move beyond their outdated strategies. This reluctance is often due to a lack of recruitment expertise among leadership and hiring teams, limited resources allocated to recruitment efforts, and resistance to adopting new methods of attracting candidates. Such a narrow approach to recruiting is a key factor in the current vacancy crisis affecting law enforcement agencies nationwide.

To attract the next generation of law enforcement leaders, agencies must embrace a visible, proactive, and strategic presence in the digital space. An effective recruitment strategy starts with understanding where potential candidates spend their time online and establishing an engaging, authentic presence on those platforms. While social media and job boards remain essential tools for reaching a broad audience, professional networking websites and online communities can also play a pivotal role in connecting with top talent. A successful strategy resonates with today's job seekers by highlighting the meaningful aspects of a law enforcement career such as public service, community impact, and opportunities for personal and professional growth. By delivering compelling and value-driven messages, agencies can inspire candidates to see law enforcement as a rewarding and purposeful path forward.

This chapter explores the strategies, best practices, and digital techniques to help law enforcement agencies create a powerful digital presence across all platforms. From leveraging social media to utilizing job boards and refining outreach campaigns, these techniques are essential to reaching candidates where they are, using a proactive approach to showcase an agency's values, mission, and vision for the future. By adopting these techniques, agencies can expand their reach and create meaningful connections with potential recruits, showing that a career in law enforcement is more than just a job. It is a purpose-driven calling.

Through these proactive digital strategies, agencies can not only improve public perception and community relationships but also inspire a new generation of officers who are motivated to serve and protect. Embracing digital platforms and a modern approach to recruitment is crucial for transforming the workforce, filling vacancies with skilled individuals who align with the mission, and ensuring law enforcement's future strength and resilience across the country.

## SOCIAL MEDIA

Social media is one of the most powerful tools in today's recruitment toolbox and should hold a significant place in your department's recruiting strategy. Social media has evolved from a place where people would simply share stories and pictures of their lives with their close friends and families to one that is utilized by every major corporation around the world. Companies use it to advertise products and services, individuals grow their personal brands, sometimes making millions of dollars in the process, and the average American spends dozens of hours a week scrolling through various social media platforms for entertainment, news, and much more. Social media has become critical for professional outreach, brand-building, and talent acquisition.

As social media has become an ever more present part of our daily lives, the law enforcement industry has been split between agencies that utilize it effectively and those that don't. Agencies that rightfully dedicate the time and resources to social media have reaped the rewards by improving community relations, receiving tips from citizens to help solve crimes, and in their recruiting efforts. Others, however, remain resistant to this form of outreach and are suffering the consequences.

Building trust with members of one community requires constant interaction, open dialogue, and the humanization of the badge. While in-person interactions are the most effective way to build positive bonds between law enforcement and their citizens, social media has become a powerful and necessary part of the process. With millions of people engaging on platforms like Facebook, Instagram, TikTok, and X daily, agencies have the opportunity to connect directly with both the public and prospective recruits in real time, offering transparency, promoting community initiatives, and showcasing the dynamic roles within law enforcement.

When used effectively, social media enables agencies to tell their stories in an authentic, engaging, and relatable way. By posting about community events, officer success stories, and the challenges and rewards of police work, agencies can humanize their departments, offering a glimpse behind the badge. This not only fosters a sense of trust within the community but also attracts recruits who are drawn to an agency's culture and values.

During my time as a Public Information Officer, I launched a weekly social media initiative called #MeetADeputyMonday. Every Monday, I would introduce a member of our agency, offering a glimpse into their journey, including what drew them to the Loudoun County Sheriff's Office and the law enforcement profession, their positions within our department, their accomplishments, and a peek into their life beyond the badge. These stories were shared across the agency's Facebook, Twitter, and Instagram accounts, and they became incredibly popular, consistently generating more reach and engagement than any other posts. It became clear that humanizing our officers profoundly impacted how the community perceived law enforcement.

Posts like #MeetADeputyMonday and those showing officers engaging in everyday acts of kindness like helping someone fix a flat tire, participating in community outreach, or showing kids around a patrol car resonated deeply with our audience. These moments captured the humanity of our officers and showed that they were more than just enforcers of the law. This kind of content went far beyond traditional PR. It offered a window into the personal and professional lives of the men and women behind the badge, strengthening the bond between our agency and the citizens we serve.

While these posts were not created specifically for recruitment, they had an undeniable effect on attracting potential candidates. With over 18,000 law enforcement agencies in the country, prospective officers are often unsure of which department to apply to. Seeing an agency that actively celebrates its members' achievements and shares personal stories can make a difference in their decisions. It gives a candidate an insight into the department's culture, showing them that this is a place where officers are valued, their contributions are recognized, and their humanity is embraced. Recruitment is not just about job postings and attending career fairs; it's about conveying the spirit of the agency and letting potential recruits see themselves as part of that culture.

Through years of research and trial and error, companies have discovered that potential customers, on average, need to see, hear, or read about products or services at least seven times before they decide to make a purchase. This is why you will see Apple advertising their latest smartphone in YouTube advertisements, on streaming platforms, on the physical signs around cities, on the radio, and in many other places in society. McDonald's has become such a regular part of our daily lives that we need only to see the golden arches or hear their "bah dah ba da da" hymn to immediately know that it's McDonald's. These organizations have teams of employees dedicated solely to ensuring their mission, purpose, and products are incredibly clear and visible to active customers and those who they have yet to draw in.

Law enforcement needs to follow a similar approach. However, instead of selling a product or service, agencies need to "sell" the exciting benefits and opportunities candidates stand to gain by becoming a member of that department. My company does consulting work with law enforcement agencies around America who need help with their recruiting and retention efforts.

In my talks with the leadership teams, I constantly stress the importance of making recruitment a continuous and agency-wide effort. Recruitment should not only happen in the months before an academy class or at a career fair, but it should become a consistent part of your agency's message. Social media has the fantastic potential to reach thousands of viewers and future candidates at little or no cost.

A 21-year-old college graduate in your jurisdiction who has decided she wants to enter the law enforcement profession should already know all about your agency after following your social media pages over the past few years. There should be no question about which agency she wants to apply to because of the engaging contact your media relations and recruiting teams have shared on your agency's social media pages.

As I shared in an earlier chapter, recruiting police officers, deputy sheriffs, correctional officers, and federal agents should include short and long-term strategies and initiatives. Sharing a social media post stating that you are actively hiring can immediately impact application numbers in the days following the post, while consistent, high-quality social media content about your agency and your staff will reap fantastic rewards in the long term as you build relationships with future candidates. We will soon discuss the importance of analytics and tracking the success of your recruiting efforts, allowing you to allocate additional resources to the most effective strategies.

I strongly encourage every law enforcement agency to transform their social media platforms into channels of engagement, going beyond serving as mere bulletin boards for crime statistics or traffic alerts. While these updates are necessary, they should not define your agency's digital presence or brand. Instead, use your agency's social media platforms as a window into the daily lives, values, and missions of the officers who serve. Highlight the extraordinary dedication your officers demonstrate every day, whether through heroic acts, routine duties, or personal milestones. Share stories that showcase their successes, community interactions, and professional growth. By doing so, your agency fosters public trust and understanding and boosts morale within the department, showing officers that their hard work is recognized and valued by leadership and the community.

Emphasizing these human-centered stories strengthens the bond between your agency and the communities you serve, cultivating a sense of unity and understanding that extends far beyond traditional law enforcement roles. Social media can reshape public perception and build a lasting foundation of trust, but only if leveraged to its fullest potential. By portraying the heart and soul of law enforcement, agencies reinforce the truth that officers are not just enforcers of the law but members of the community dedicated to its well-being. This approach is especially crucial in attracting new candidates, often drawn to agencies that demonstrate a deep commitment to transparency, engagement, and community values. Through authentic storytelling, your department can become an aspirational example of community-centered policing.

Moreover, the interactive nature of social media provides an invaluable opportunity for direct dialogue with the public. Open and honest communication is essential for fostering community trust and support. The era when law enforcement could operate in secrecy with little explanation to the public is long gone. Citizens today expect and demand transparency and accountability.

Social media allows community members to ask questions, express concerns, and feel genuinely heard. Many citizens are eager to understand what their local, state, and federal agencies are doing to ensure their safety and support their community. Most individuals have not served as officers and may have concerns or curiosities that can be alleviated with straightforward, respectful communication. Addressing these through open channels on social media can bridge gaps in understanding and build a foundation of mutual respect and trust.

Law enforcement agencies have historically relied on traditional community engagement methods, such as in-person meetings and media interactions. While these approaches were effective in their time, the evolving communication landscape demands a strategic shift to reach younger generations who are more digitally connected. Without a robust and dynamic social media presence, these audiences are unlikely to engage with law enforcement's messaging or initiatives.

For instance, my agency hosted quarterly meetings at its four substations, where station commanders discussed crime trends, community events, and other topics of interest. Despite significant efforts, attendance at these events was consistently poor, with most participants being in their 40s, 50s, or older. Virtually no one from the younger generation attended. This disconnect underscores the need for law enforcement to rethink their engagement strategies.

Agencies must invest in vibrant, interactive social media platforms that foster genuine dialogue. These platforms shouldn't just provide updates but serve as spaces where citizens feel empowered to ask questions, share concerns, and connect with the human side of policing. Building these connections is critical for fostering trust and understanding with future generations.

By cultivating an interactive, accessible online presence, law enforcement agencies foster trust and transparency and enable citizens to become active participants in their community's safety and well-being. A robust social media campaign is an opportunity to showcase your team's daily work, dedication, and professionalism and demonstrate your commitment to openness and accountability. Through genuine engagement, your agency can strengthen relationships with all age groups, particularly younger citizens who value transparency and are highly engaged online.

When I see agencies disabling the ability for citizens to comment on their social media posts because of a few negative remarks, I feel a deep sense of frustration. Social media offers a rare and direct channel for law enforcement to engage openly with the communities they serve. By shutting down comments, agencies are silencing critics and missing invaluable opportunities for dialogue with supporters and neutral parties alike. Closing off communication because of a handful of harsh remarks limits the potential for public trust and accountability, sending an unintended message that the agency is not open to feedback.

The law enforcement profession has been under intense scrutiny for a long time, often facing criticism and misunderstandings from those unfamiliar with or opposed to the critical role officers play. Such scrutiny comes with the territory of serving in a public-facing role. Dissenting voices, while sometimes harsh, can offer valuable insights into community concerns. Instead of halting the conversation, agencies should seize the opportunity to engage with critics respectfully, addressing misinformation with facts and demonstrating the professionalism and commitment of law enforcement. This approach not only diffuses tensions but also shows a commitment to fairness and responsiveness, even to those who may disagree with policing practices.

I firmly believe that the negative voices criticizing law enforcement, no matter how loud or pervasive they may seem, represent only a small fraction of the public. The vast majority of people respect and support law enforcement, even if they don't always express it openly. By maintaining open social media channels that welcome all viewpoints, positive and negative, agencies provide a platform where the supportive majority can step forward and share their appreciation. This openness sends a powerful message that law enforcement is accountable, transparent, and ready to engage in meaningful, honest dialogue with the communities they serve.

Such transparency does more than build trust. It strengthens the foundation of effective community policing by fostering integrity and accessibility. It also plays a crucial role in improving recruitment and retention within law enforcement. When agencies nurture positive relationships with the public and actively dispel the misconception that society is broadly anti-law enforcement, they create an environment where officers feel valued and supported. This effort helps attract new talent and reinforces the morale of those already serving, ensuring a stronger, more connected future for the profession.

## NO ONE-TRICK PONY

Social media is continuously evolving, as are the ways people consume and create content. Historically, Facebook, Twitter, and Instagram posts focused heavily on pictures and text, but with the rise of platforms like YouTube and TikTok, video has quickly become the preferred content for a broad demographic of social media users.

Even LinkedIn, a platform traditionally geared toward text-based professional networking, has shifted toward video content, recognizing its value in reaching wider audiences. The algorithms that drive what users see are now prioritizing video, both short and long form, over traditional photo and text posts. This trend means that if law enforcement agencies want to remain relevant and visible, they must embrace video content.

Platforms like YouTube, TikTok, and Instagram Reels offer law enforcement agencies powerful tools to create visually engaging recruitment content that showcases everything from "day-in-the-life" vlogs to the rigorous training required to become an officer and much more. Videos are uniquely capable of capturing attention and forging emotional connections, making them an ideal medium for attracting prospective recruits. Well-produced recruitment videos can portray the mental, physical, and emotional aspects of law enforcement work, communicating the realities of the job in ways that static posts cannot.

Law enforcement agencies, however, have traditionally been slow to adopt video-based outreach. This is evident in the sparse and often low-quality video content produced by departments across America. Security and confidentiality are certainly significant concerns, but the primary barriers to video content appear to be limited resources, insufficient training, a lack of understanding of the true power of video content, and the convenience of simpler picture-and-text posts. However, with a small investment of time, training, and funding, agencies could be equipped to create impactful video content that resonates with their communities and sets them apart from others.

Contrary to popular belief, creating quality video content doesn't require thousands of dollars or a degree in film production. Most videos seen on social media today are filmed on smartphones using affordable video kits that include basic lighting, a phone holder, and a microphone. Basic versions of these items can be purchased as a bundle for under $100. Video editing software ranges from free

COLIN WHITTINGTON

versions for basic edits to affordable advanced software, which can meet the needs of nearly any law enforcement project. Fantastic video content doesn't need to cost your agency a fortune. Additionally, virtual and in-person training courses on filming, editing, and sharing video content are widely available, allowing your staff to gain the essential skills to produce engaging video content quickly. With a modest initial investment, agencies can transform their content strategy, drawing their audience into a more immersive experience and showcasing aspects of the job that are best conveyed through video.

Shows like Cops and Live PD have gained immense popularity because people are naturally curious about what officers do on a daily basis. Your agency could create similar behind-the-scenes content highlighting law enforcement's diverse responsibilities and opportunities. For example, a public information officer could film a "day in the life" with a patrol officer, capturing moments from morning roll calls to coffee breaks, traffic stops, emergency responses, and community interactions. Such a video would not only be engaging for the public but also provide potential recruits with a realistic look into the daily life of an officer, making it a powerful recruiting tool as well.

Other ideas include filming forensic teams in action, showcasing K-9 units during training, or featuring your Search and Rescue team using the latest technology. While sharing a post with photos and texts for these events will attract some attention, a video can capture the dynamic nature of these events, creating a strong connection with viewers and giving them a firsthand look at your team's dedication and skills.

To further enhance recruitment efforts, consider hosting live Q&A sessions with the chief or sheriff and recruiting team members. These sessions offer a unique opportunity to interact directly with prospective candidates, allowing them to ask questions about the agency, the recruitment process, benefits, and more. This approach makes candidates feel more informed and demonstrates that the agency's leadership values recruitment and is willing to engage with candidates directly. With platforms like Microsoft Teams or Zoom, hosting such virtual events is simple and free. Agencies can announce the Q&A on their social media channels, collect interested candidates' names and emails, and send them a link to join. By doing so, the agency can build a database of contacts for potential follow-ups and have an opportunity to make initial impressions of prospective candidates without traveling great distances to career fairs or other in-person events.

Through consistent and well-curated video content, law enforcement agencies can foster a more engaging, accessible, and appealing digital presence. Virtual "job fairs," where your department is the main focus, make it easier to connect with top-tier candidates and ensure a cost-effective and impactful recruitment strategy. Embracing the full potential of video content on social media strengthens community relationships and ensures that the agency remains competitive and relevant in a digital-first world.

## LINKEDIN

While every social media platform can play a valuable role in an agency's recruitment strategy, LinkedIn stands out as a crucial yet underutilized tool with transformative potential for law enforcement recruitment. Nearly every major organization, corporation, and non-profit leverage LinkedIn to connect with candidates and share information and stories. Law enforcement, however, has been slower in recognizing LinkedIn's potential. In my opinion, this is a missed opportunity. With over 900 million users, LinkedIn offers an expansive and diverse talent pool: professionals exploring new paths, open to unique challenges, or interested in a career that makes a meaningful difference. For agencies eager to attract top-tier candidates, LinkedIn provides an invaluable opportunity to broaden their reach and engage with potential recruits in ways that extend beyond traditional hiring methods.

When I took over the Employment Services Section at the Loudoun County Sheriff's Office, one of my top priorities was to modernize our recruitment efforts by establishing an official agency LinkedIn Company Page. Like many people, I created a LinkedIn profile during a college course but rarely used in the years that followed graduation. I did not take the time to get to know the platform or recognize the benefit it could have on my career. However, with my new role came a fresh perspective, and I soon recognized the platform's immense potential as a strategic tool for law enforcement recruitment. I saw an opportunity to showcase our agency's unique strengths and create a pipeline of high-quality candidates by leveraging LinkedIn's reach and professional networking capabilities.

Like any new initiative in law enforcement, launching our LinkedIn Company Page required thorough research, data, and a clear plan before obtaining leadership approval. Over the following weeks, I immersed myself in the platform, studying its features and capabilities and developing a targeted strategy. I was surprised to learn that very few law enforcement agencies were active on LinkedIn. On the other hand, companies across various private sector industries routinely shared job postings, highlighted employee achievements, and engaged in industry-specific conversations. I saw professionals from all backgrounds sharing their stories, looking for new opportunities, and asking questions. The potential to reach such a wide and diverse talent pool was unmistakable. I believe LinkedIn could be a game-changer for our recruitment efforts.

LinkedIn's unique professional focus enables law enforcement agencies to cultivate authentic relationships with prospective recruits. Unlike other platforms such as Facebook, X, Instagram, and TikTok, LinkedIn is tailored for job searching, networking, and professional conversations.

While those other social media sites are primarily used for entertainment, many users on LinkedIn are actively seeking new roles or passively open to career opportunities, presenting law enforcement with a unique opportunity to recruit and build an authentic department brand. By showcasing the agency's values, mission, and the meaningful work officers perform every day, law enforcement agencies can reach individuals who may not have previously considered a career in public service. This professionalism and commitment to law and order can shine on LinkedIn, making the platform particularly appealing to those open to exploring new career paths.

One of LinkedIn's greatest assets is its capacity to help agencies build a brand that resonates with a broad professional audience. Law enforcement agencies can use LinkedIn to share updates on community initiatives, highlight success stories, promote benefits, and showcase career development opportunities. In an era where younger generations prioritize purpose-driven careers, this approach helps agencies attract individuals committed to making a positive impact. As discussed in Chapter 3, today's workforce actively seeks employers who are aligned with their values. With LinkedIn, agencies can present themselves as progressive, community-focused organizations that offer public service and a workplace committed to the growth and well-being of its officers.

Additionally, LinkedIn fosters professional conversations around topics like criminal justice, community safety, and leadership development. Through LinkedIn Groups, communities where professionals with shared interests connect, exchange insights, and discuss relevant topics, law enforcement agencies can join or initiate discussions within circles dedicated to these themes. This can position the agency as a thought leader and enable potential candidates to engage directly with agency representatives. Such interaction offers candidates a more personal understanding of the agency's values, mission, and culture. By dispelling common misconceptions about the profession, LinkedIn allows candidates to envision a future where they join a team dedicated to service, integrity, and personal growth.

For agencies willing to explore LinkedIn's potential fully, the platform provides a powerful way to connect with quality candidates, expand the agency's influence, and inspire professionals seeking purposeful work to consider law enforcement as a career path. Law enforcement agencies can utilize LinkedIn to build a sustainable recruitment pipeline that aligns with the evolving demands of today's workforce. By consistently posting updates, participating in conversations, and sharing agency values, departments are able to engage with their followers and potential recruits. Law enforcement can and should embrace LinkedIn not only as a tool for hiring but also as a strategic channel for future growth, community building, and establishing a resilient, mission-driven workforce.

Despite the undeniable potential, it's surprising how few law enforcement agencies utilize LinkedIn effectively or at all. Many agencies have robust social media presence on Facebook, X, or Instagram but fail to recognize the benefits of LinkedIn, a platform dedicated exclusively to working professionals. LinkedIn's limited law enforcement representation creates an excellent opportunity for agencies willing to embrace it. By consistently engaging on LinkedIn, your agency can differentiate itself and attract attention from candidates actively seeking meaningful and stable careers. If your agency does not yet have a LinkedIn presence, it's time to prioritize it for your recruiting and hiring teams.

Fortunately, my agency was very receptive to the idea of starting a Loudoun County Sheriff's Office Company Page. After gaining the necessary approvals, I quickly went to work to create our profile. I began implementing a strategy to regularly post job opportunities, respond to questions, and engage with candidates. The entire set-up process cost the agency nothing but my time and attention, yet it yielded incredible results. In just over two and a half years, our agency's LinkedIn page grew to the largest law enforcement LinkedIn page in Virginia, and a remarkable 40% of all our applicants reported discovering our agency through LinkedIn. While many departments were spending tens of thousands of dollars on various recruitment-related initiatives, we found wonderful success by simply telling our story, engaging with potential candidates, and sharing what they had to gain by joining our organization.

I believe that your agency can replicate this success when launching your LinkedIn page. Remember, though, that LinkedIn's potential for recruitment depends entirely on the dedication and consistency of your team's efforts. Posting sporadically will not drive significant engagement or help your department stand out in a competitive job market. To see real results, assign the responsibility to someone passionate about recruitment and digital outreach, whether a recruiter, a public information officer, or any individual with a vested interest in expanding your department's online presence. With regular, thoughtful content and a clear strategy, your agency's LinkedIn page can become a powerful tool for finding and attracting the right candidates.

Setting up your agency's LinkedIn Company Page is straightforward, yet the long-term benefits are immense. Here's a roadmap to leverage LinkedIn's power for your agency's recruiting efforts. This guide will help you create a page showcasing your department, attracting quality candidates, and building a professional network.

## STEP 1: OBTAIN APPROVALS

- **Discuss Goals:** Meet with your department's leadership to discuss the value of a LinkedIn presence, explaining how it can attract applicants and improve community outreach at little to no cost to the agency.

- **Get Approvals:** Make sure you have formal approval to represent your agency on LinkedIn and post on behalf of the department. Depending on your agency's situation, creating a LinkedIn profile may also require town, city, county, or state governmental approval. Make sure everyone is on the same page and fully aware of what is required to create and maintain a LinkedIn Company Page.

## STEP 2: PREPARE YOUR CONTENT AND VISUALS

- **Gather Materials:** To create a successful LinkedIn Company page, you will need various images, texts, and information about your agency. Collect your department's logo, high-quality photos, and relevant details such as the agency's history, mission, and values. Ensure that the appropriate authorities also approve all these items.

- **Draft an "About" Section:** One of the key elements of a LinkedIn Company Page is the "About" section, also known as the overview section. Write a brief, engaging description of your department. Include your mission, the communities you serve, and what makes your department unique. I like to include a message from the highest-ranking member of your agency, typically the chief or sheriff. This message should be directed toward potential candidates, highlighting the leader's commitment and passion for hiring and what candidates stand to gain by joining your organization. Currently, LinkedIn's overview section may contain up to 2,000 characters.

- **Plan Your First Few Posts:** Having a plan for the first few weeks of your agency's LinkedIn page allows you to feel prepared and have a well-thought-out plan in place. Prepare introductory posts that might highlight your agency's values, showcase the team, and include any current job openings.

## STEP 3: SET UP THE LINKEDIN COMPANY PAGE

- **Login to LinkedIn:** To create a LinkedIn Company Page, the creator must sign into his or her personal LinkedIn account. It is currently impossible for someone without a LinkedIn account to create a Company Page. The person who creates the account will be assigned the title of "Super Admin," the highest authority of that company page. This position can edit the profile, share posts, invite other "Admins," and establish their authorizations for the account. These positions can all be changed at any time in the Account Settings tab.

- Create the Page:
  - Select "Work" on the top-right of LinkedIn.
  - Scroll down and click on "Create a Company Page."
  - Choose "Company. Small, medium, and large business." There is no option for government agency.

- Enter Basic Details:
  - **Logo:** Add a high-resolution image of your department's logo.

  - **Page Identity:** Enter your agency name and a custom URL, for example, "linkedin.com/company/YourAgencyName." I recommend using your agency's full, official name. I suggest not including the acronym, as that makes the title appear too busy and not as clean.

  - **Tagline:** The tagline, also referred to as the Headline appears directly below your agency's logo. It can only be up to 120 characters long, so be intentional with your word choice. When I created the Company Page for the Loudoun County Sheriff's Office, I came up with this tagline: "The largest, full-service Sheriff's Office in Virginia, dedicated to serving the citizens of Loudoun County."

  - **Website:** Include your agency's website. If you have a separate careers/recruiting page or website, I recommend using that page or website since most visitors will be candidates looking for more information on your agency's career opportunities.

  - **Industry:** Choose "Law Enforcement" or "Public Safety."

  - **Organization Size:** Select the appropriate option based on the number of personnel in your agency. Include both sworn and civilian staff members.

  - **Organization Type:** Choose "government agency"

- Customize the Page:
  - **About Us/Overview:** Add the agency description you prepared. As I mentioned earlier, this section gives you the opportunity to highlight what makes your agency unique, the opportunities you can provide interested candidates, a message from your chief or sheriff, and more. Make this section as strong as you possibly can!

  - **Location:** Enter your department's location(s). If you have several locations, such as headquarters, substations, and adult detention centers, I suggest entering a location for each facility. Be sure to label the type of location for each.

- **Specialties:** Add key areas of focus, such as "Community Policing," "K-9," "Crisis Intervention Team," "SWAT," and "Criminal Investigations Division." Remember, your page will be viewed by Millennials and Gen Z, who value career growth opportunities. Highlighting their options for a diverse career with your agency will significantly enhance your recruiting abilities. You can share up to 20 specialties on your agency's page.

■ **Save and Publish:** Review everything, then hit "Create Page." Congratulations, your page is now live!

## STEP 4: COMPLETE YOUR PROFILE WITH A COVER IMAGE AND ADDITIONAL DETAILS

■ **Cover Image:** The cover image is the rectangular-shaped image that is displayed behind your agency's logo. This is an excellent place to share an image of your officers, a community event, a notable landmark in your jurisdiction, a cruiser, or a similar type of picture. The dimensions for this image are 1,128px x 191px. You can utilize free websites such as Canva.com to create a LinkedIn Cover/Background image. Then, upload the high-resolution image to your agency's Company Page.

■ Additional Sections:
- **Workplace:** This section allows organizations to share whether their employees work on-site, hybrid, or remote. As a law enforcement agency, most of your employees will probably be on-site, which won't surprise most candidates considering a career in law enforcement.

- **Commitments:** Law enforcement agencies can leverage the Commitments section of their LinkedIn company page to showcase their dedication to values that resonate with potential recruits, such as community service, work-life balance, and professional development. By detailing specific programs, initiatives, and training opportunities that support these values, agencies can demonstrate their commitment to fostering a positive work environment and a culture of continuous growth. Highlighting community engagement projects, outreach to underserved populations, and initiatives for officer wellness can appeal to recruits looking for an agency that prioritizes public service and its personnel's well-being.

## STEP 5: BUILD OUT INITIAL CONTENT

- **Introduce the Page:** After all your hard work, your page is finally live, and you want the world to know! Create a welcome post introducing your agency's LinkedIn page and inviting people to follow it for updates, news, and job openings. Inform your staff about the page, encourage them to follow it, and tag the agency's page on their work experience section on their personal LinkedIn profiles. We will soon discuss the topic of making every member of your agency an unofficial recruiter and the incredible impact they can have on your recruiting efforts. Having them participate in advancing the agency's LinkedIn page is an excellent place to start.

- **Highlight Team Members and Roles:** Post about different roles within the department and members of your team. This should not only include command staff members, though you do want to highlight them, too. You should highlight your officers, detectives, and even administrative staff. One of the greatest ways to humanize the badge and increase application numbers is by highlighting and recognizing your staff. Not only does this allow candidates to learn about the various positions available to them with your department, but it also allows them to envision working in the law enforcement profession when they see others with similar backgrounds already doing so.

- **Share Community Involvement:** A major part of a successful recruiting strategy is building an agency "brand." Your brand is developed over weeks, months, and years of consistently highlighting your mission, values, and purpose in the community.

LinkedIn can be a powerful place to develop and utilize your brand to improve your recruiting numbers. Post regularly about the department's involvement in community events, charity work, and safety programs. This type of content can have both immediate and long-term impacts on recruitment.

## STEP 6: DEVELOP A POSTING SCHEDULE

- **Frequency:** To ensure your agency's page remains visible, plan to share posts at least two or three times a week. Fortunately, a lot of the content your agency shares on other social media platforms like Facebook, X, and Instagram can also be shared on LinkedIn, which will save you time. However, you should aim to make at least one recruitment-specific post a week for your agency's LinkedIn page.

- **Content Types:** Mix up your content with job postings, stories from current officers, training highlights, and recruitment tips. Being repetitive will result in decreased engagement and a lack of growth. Share images and videos, write longer articles about a law enforcement-related topic, ask questions that can lead to engagement from potential recruits, and host live Q&A sessions. Make your department's profile a place people want to go to in order to learn more about law enforcement and your agency.

- **Engage with Followers:** One of the reasons my department's LinkedIn profile was so successful was that I took the time to answer every comment and question our followers posed. Respond to comments and messages you receive. Engagement shows potential applicants that the department is approachable and invested in its community. This goes back to the topic of reactive vs. proactive recruitment. To successfully recruit for law enforcement in this current climate, agencies must take more significant steps than ever to attract candidates to their organizations.

## STEP 7: TRACK AND MEASURE ENGAGEMENT

- **Use LinkedIn Analytics:** I will discuss the importance of metrics and tracking Key Performance Indicators (KPIs) throughout this book. Recruiting is an ever-evolving process. Your agency should constantly look for ways to improve and be more efficient with your efforts. Monitor the analytics on your LinkedIn page to understand which posts get the most views and engagement. Over time, you will start to see a trend in what type of content is successful and what is less so.

- **Adjust Content Based on Metrics:** Refine your content strategy using insights from the metrics and data on your company page. If recruitment posts gain the most engagement, consider increasing their frequency. If your followers love hearing about your officers, work to share more stories about your staff. If content shared in the morning hours performs better than posts published in the afternoon, make it a priority to post in the morning.

## STEP 8: PROMOTE THE PAGE

- **Encourage Team Involvement:** Ask department members to follow the page, share posts, and help spread the word.

- **Cross-Promote on Other Platforms:** Add the link to your LinkedIn page on your department's other social media accounts. This is useful for agencies with large followings on other platforms as it will also help to grow your LinkedIn profile. Include the link to your LinkedIn page and all your agency's social media platforms on the department's website. Finally, you can consider adding a link to the agency's profile on employees' email signatures, making every email sent a potential recruiting tool for your department.

## STEP 9: MAINTAIN AND OPTIMIZE

- **Stay Consistent:** Regular, engaging content keeps followers invested and helps attract new ones. It's easy to be motivated in the early weeks and months of having the platform. However, to make LinkedIn a significant part of your recruitment strategy, you must maintain consistency and build followership over time.

■ **Respond to Comments:** This point is worth repeating. I see it as a significantly missed opportunity when law enforcement agencies fail to respond to comments or questions on their social media platforms. Not only is responding to comments the polite thing to do, but it can also encourage ongoing interaction and show the platform's algorithm that your posts create engagement and conversation, resulting in a wider audience seeing your posts. Take the time to respond to all comments.

With these steps, your agency can leverage LinkedIn not just to find candidates but to foster a long-lasting connection with the community and build a reputable brand image. In a field where positive public perception is paramount, LinkedIn is a powerful tool that provides direct access to future law enforcement officers and community supporters.

The time has come for law enforcement to fully embrace LinkedIn, transforming it into a cornerstone of modern recruiting strategy. With intentional use and consistent engagement, LinkedIn can significantly broaden your agency's outreach, attract qualified, value-driven recruits, and build a network that will continue to benefit your department for years to come. By prioritizing LinkedIn alongside other recruiting efforts, your agency can set a new standard in law enforcement recruitment and effectively tap into a wider, more diverse talent pool.

Ultimately, LinkedIn is more than just a job board. It is a platform that offers law enforcement agencies the ability to connect with talent, engage with their community, and enhance their overall recruitment strategy. As the largest professional network in the world, LinkedIn gives agencies the chance to showcase their department, highlight career opportunities, and attract qualified candidates who are eager to make a difference. By leveraging this tool to its full potential, law enforcement agencies can modernize their recruitment efforts and build a more diverse, skilled, and engaged workforce for the future.

## PAID ADVERTISING

Social media is an excellent space for law enforcement agencies to grow their brand, connect with citizens, and build a sustained recruiting strategy. One of the best parts of social media is that so much of it can be done entirely for free. All it takes is a bit of creativity and effort to reap big rewards. However, it is also a powerful arena for dedicating some of your agency's budget toward targeted recruitment campaigns to accelerate recruitment and hiring. With advertising tools built into platforms like Facebook, Instagram, and LinkedIn, agencies can run ads crafted explicitly for those interested in criminal justice, community service, or public safety careers. These tools allow agencies to fine-tune their ads to reach specific demographics, geographic areas, and individuals with certain educational backgrounds or career experiences. The ability to precisely segment and target audiences helps ensure that your recruitment messages connect with candidates who align with your department's mission and values.

Traditional media outlets like television, newspapers, and radio can undoubtedly reach large audiences. However, as discussed in an earlier chapter, there are fundamental drawbacks to recruiting for law enforcement careers utilizing those outlets. Those audiences are often broad and lack specificity. Many viewers or listeners will have no interest in or connection to law enforcement, resulting in wasted exposure, diluted impacts, and a drain on your funding. In contrast, social media advertising enables a laser-focused approach by allowing you to target specific audiences based on their demographics, interests, and even online behavior. This targeted reach maximizes your recruitment budget, ensuring that your message appears directly in front of people who are more likely to be interested and may already be considering careers in law enforcement. Social media advertising should be about precision rather than volume, making your investment more efficient and effective.

Social media advertising offers a unique opportunity to reach new audiences who may have never encountered your agency before.

While regularly posting engaging content is a valuable strategy for building your brand, fostering credibility, and nurturing relationships with existing followers, it has limitations. Organic posts primarily reach those who already follow your account, and even then, only a small fraction of your followers will see your content due to algorithm restrictions. This is akin to speaking to an audience that already knows you rather than introducing yourself to new potential supporters or recruits. While consistent, high-quality organic content is an excellent long-term strategy for growing your audience, its impact on expanding your reach is gradual.

Paid social media advertising, on the other hand, breaks through these barriers. It allows your agency to connect with individuals who align with your ideal candidate profile but have yet to discover the opportunities you offer. These people represent untapped potential. They could be the dedicated recruits you're searching for, but without targeted outreach, they may never cross paths with your agency. Social media advertising bridges this gap, generating awareness and sparking interest among fresh, highly targeted audiences.

Through these advertising campaigns, you can showcase your agency's mission, values, and career opportunities to a broader, previously untapped demographic. By targeting specific attributes such as interests, education, and professional backgrounds, you can engage individuals who may not be actively job hunting but are likely to resonate with your message and consider law enforcement as a potential career path. This strategic outreach broadens your candidate pool and lays the foundation for meaningful relationships, planting seeds of interest that can grow into genuine engagement and future recruitment success.

One of the most significant advantages of social media advertising is its budget flexibility. You have complete control over your daily spending, whether you start with just five dollars per day or go all-in with a larger budget of hundreds or even thousands of dollars. As recruiting budgets vary greatly from agency to agency, this flexibility accommodates a range of financial capabilities, making social

COLIN WHITTINGTON

media advertising accessible to agencies and organizations of all sizes. Unlike traditional media, where the cost is often fixed and substantial, social media platforms let you scale your spending to match your goals and resources.

Starting with a smaller daily budget offers the strategic advantage of experimenting and gathering valuable insights without a significant upfront investment. You can test different messaging styles, audience segments, and ad formats with just a few dollars to see what resonates best with your target candidates. You may find that one image draws more attention than another or that video content drives more traffic to your website than text. This experimentation phase allows you to observe engagement patterns and identify the elements that yield the strongest responses, making future campaigns more targeted and effective.

As your campaign unfolds, the option to adjust your budget in real time becomes invaluable. If a particular ad performs well, you can easily allocate more funds to boost its reach and impact. Conversely, if an approach isn't hitting the mark, you can reduce the budget or pause the ad, saving resources and shifting focus to strategies that generate better results. This adaptability ensures you're never locked into a campaign that isn't delivering.

For those new to social media advertising, I recommend starting with a small daily budget while familiarizing yourself with the platform's features and audience insights. Take time to learn how different targeting options, ad placements, and content styles affect engagement. Gradually, as you become more comfortable and recognize strategies that effectively capture your audience's attention, you can confidently increase your investment to expand your reach and achieve greater impact.

By taking this phased approach, you can maximize your return on investment while building a strong foundation in social media advertising. Starting small and scaling up as you learn lets you allocate resources wisely, leading to more refined campaigns and successful outreach efforts.

Another key advantage to paid advertising is the availability of detailed, real-time analytics. Before your campaign even launches, social media platforms provide estimated reach metrics that give you a preview of the potential audience size based on your targeting and budget choices. These estimates allow you to gauge the effectiveness of your parameters in advance, helping you make informed decisions before any money is spent. By knowing how many people are likely to see your ad and how many are expected to click on your website, you can plan your campaign's impact more effectively and make necessary adjustments to meet your agency's goals.

Once the campaign is live, you can access real-time statistics showing exactly how your ad is performing. This transparency is invaluable because it allows you to track your advertisement's reach, engagement rates, and other critical metrics as they happen. Instead of waiting until a campaign concludes to assess its effectiveness, which is often the case with traditional media, you can immediately see whether your message resonates with your target audience. This real-time feedback loop is crucial in refining your approach, as it lets you make informed, timely adjustments to ensure you're getting the best possible results.

This combination of flexible spending, detailed pre-campaign estimates, and real-time tracking gives you unparalleled control over your advertising efforts. You can continuously optimize your campaign's reach and impact by making adjustments that align with your objectives while stretching your budget further. Social media advertising's adaptability and transparency mean you can maximize every dollar spent, ensuring your message reaches the right people without the waste often associated with traditional advertising methods.

# SOCIAL MEDIA ADVERTISING TERMS

When you first start utilizing social media advertising to bolster your agency's recruiting efforts, you will see a variety of terms that you may be unfamiliar with. Don't let these intimidate you. Here are some of the most important terms you will see on social media advertising, statistics you'll want to track, and how you can work to improve them to make your advertisement more effective:

1. **Impressions**

■ **Description:** Impressions represent the number of times your ad is displayed to users on that particular social media platform. An impression is counted each time an ad appears on a user's screen, regardless of whether they engage with it. You know the advertisements you see while scrolling through Facebook? Each time you see one, you are counted as an impression in that company's advertising campaign.

■ **How to Track:** Most social media platforms offer real-time tracking of impressions through their analytics dashboards, allowing you to monitor how frequently your ad is shown over a campaign period.

■ **Improvement Tips:** To increase impressions, consider adjusting your ad budget or targeting broader audiences. Posting at peak times when your audience is most active and using eye-catching visuals and clear messaging can also boost impressions. While impression numbers are certainly a factor in an ad's success, some of the terms I'll be describing next are far more important in ensuring an effective campaign. After all, it doesn't do you much good if thousands of people see your advertisement and simply scroll on without interacting with it.

2. **Reach**

■ **Description:** Reach measures the unique number of people who have seen your ad at least once. Unlike impressions, reach only counts unique views, so one person viewing the ad multiple times is counted as one reach. This gives you a more accurate picture of how many people have seen your ad.

- **How to Track:** Platforms like Facebook and LinkedIn display reach metrics in campaign analytics. Comparing reach to impressions helps you understand whether your ad is being repeatedly shown to the same people or to new viewers. If your impressions are significantly higher than your reach, it's a sign that your advertisement is being repeatedly shown to the same people.

- **Improvement Tip:** Expand your reach by fine-tuning your targeting to include relevant audience segments you may not have initially considered, such as recent graduates in criminal justice fields or those who follow certain law enforcement groups on the platform. Increasing your budget or ad placement options can also help reach a wider audience.

3. **Click-Through Rate (CTR)**

- **Description:** CTR is the percentage of people who clicked on your ad after seeing it. It's calculated by dividing the total number of clicks by the number of impressions, reflecting how engaging your ad content is to viewers. A good click-through rate (CTR) depends on the platform and ad type, but here are some general benchmarks:

  - **Facebook and Instagram Ads:** 0.9% to 1.6% is considered average for most industries. Law enforcement or public service ads might see similar CTRs, though some targeted ads have performed slightly better due to local relevance and community interest.

  - **LinkedIn Ads:** LinkedIn tends to have lower CTRs, with averages between 0.4% and 0.6%, as it's more niche and often used for professional networking rather than social browsing. From my experience, ads targeting specific job roles perform better, so be sure to create an advertisement for a particular role rather than one about your agency in general.

- **Google Search Ads:** Google Search ads typically have higher CTRs, averaging around 2% to 3%, because these ads appear in search results and often respond to a user's active search intent.

- **Instagram:** On Instagram, a good click-through rate generally ranges from 0.5% to 1.5%, depending on the type of ad, the target audience, and the industry. For highly engaging or targeted ads, CTRs may sometimes exceed 2%.

■ **How to Track**: Social media dashboards automatically display your CTR. Compare your CTR with industry benchmarks to gauge performance.

■ **Improvement Tips:** To improve CTR, use compelling visuals, strong calls to action, and engaging language that resonates with your target audience. Experimenting with different ad formats, such as videos or carousel ads, can also help boost CTR. A good CTR often exceeds the industry average and signals that the ad content and targeting are well-aligned with the audience's interests. If you spend time carefully selecting your target audience, I am confident you can exceed these numbers. Generally, anything above 1% on social media and above 3% on search ads is a strong CTR, indicating high engagement and relevance to the audience.

4. **Cost Per Click (CPC)**

■ **Description:** CPC is the amount you pay each time someone clicks on your ad. A lower CPC indicates your ad is efficient in generating interest, while a higher CPC may signal that the ad content or targeting needs adjustment. A good CPC ranges from $1.50 on Facebook and Instagram to $5.00 on LinkedIn. You shouldn't be discouraged or intimidated by a higher CPC on LinkedIn, as the platform offers precise targeting to reach highly qualified candidates, such as individuals with relevant degrees or those open to new career opportunities, things not as effectively done on other platforms. While LinkedIn's CPC may be higher, the platform's professional environment means clicks are more likely to come from serious, high-quality applicants, making each click more valuable. Additionally, LinkedIn's tools allow agencies to reach experienced officers or career changers actively looking for roles in public service, maximizing recruitment efforts and potentially reducing time-to-hire.

- **How to Track:** CPC is automatically tracked in your ad's budget section. Monitoring CPC over time can help assess cost efficiency and adjust spending if needed.

- **Improvement Tips:** Reduce CPC by narrowing your audience to a more specific group and refining ad copy to match their interests. Regularly testing different images, headlines, and calls-to-action can lower CPC by making your ad more attractive to the right viewers. While doing so may reduce your overall impressions and reach, you will see an improvement in CPC, a far more critical metric.

5. **Cost Per Thousand Impressions (CPM)**

- **Description:** CPM represents the cost of 1,000 impressions of your ad. It's commonly used in brand awareness campaigns where reaching a large number of people is a priority. This will help you see how much your advertisement is costing you, allowing you to determine its effectiveness regarding your overall budget and recruiting plan.

- **How to Track:** CPM is visible in most ad dashboards under budget metrics. It can help you compare the cost-effectiveness of campaigns with similar goals. As I'll show you shortly, I recommend agencies run several campaigns simultaneously. This allows you to compare different metrics, including CPM, to determine which advertisement is having the biggest impact on viewers. You can then pause lower-performing campaigns and add additional finances for those that are performing well.

- **Improvement Tips:** Lowering your campaign's CPM can often be achieved by broadening your audience or enhancing the ad's relevance. If your target audience is extremely narrow, costs per impression can climb as you reach a smaller pool of users.

However, if the ad effectively brings a steady flow of quality applicants, don't let a slightly higher CPM overshadow its success. For instance, even if your campaign's CPM is $7 compared to Facebook's average of $6, the return on investment remains impressive if it drives qualified applicants to your department. You can still work to improve your CPM by ensuring you use high-quality visuals and well-tailored messaging. This will make your ads more attractive, encouraging engagement and expanding the reach within your target audience.

6. **Engagement Rate**

■ **Description:** Engagement rate is a metric that measures the total interactions (likes, comments, shares, etc.) on your ad, divided by its total reach. A high engagement rate shows that your audience finds the content relevant and compelling enough to interact with, which reflects positively on your campaign's appeal. In both law enforcement recruitment and corporate advertising, the most effective campaigns spark conversations, raise awareness, and encourage viewer interaction. Each like, comment, and share amplifies the ad's visibility and widens its reach as it draws in additional viewers who may also engage with it, creating a ripple effect. Think about your experience on social media: posts with high engagement are naturally more eye-catching and likely to hold your attention than those without interaction. Engaging content has the power to create momentum, making it a valuable tool for reaching and resonating with potential applicants.

■ **How to Track:** Engagement rate is typically tracked in the analytics section. Comparing engagement rates across different ads can reveal which types of content resonate best. From my experience, campaigns that had higher engagement rates also had a significantly higher number of people who visited my website or application page.

■ **Improvement Tips:** Increase engagement by incorporating interactive and inviting elements into your posts. Try asking open-ended questions, like "What qualities do you think make

COLIN WHITTINGTON

a great officer?" or adding calls to action inviting viewers to participate, such as "Share with someone who would make a fantastic addition to our team." Storytelling can also play a powerful role in capturing attention. Consider posting stories or videos highlighting the experiences of real officers, showcasing their daily contributions and the positive impact they have on the community. This type of authentic, human-centered content enhances engagement and builds a stronger connection with potential recruits drawn to meaningful service.

7. **Conversion Rate**

- **Description:** Conversion rate measures the percentage of people who complete the desired action, such as signing up for an event, downloading an information packet, or visiting a careers page after clicking on your ad. A high conversion rate suggests the ad is reaching qualified leads who are motivated to engage further. If you have a campaign specifically aimed at recruiting applicants for police officer positions and notice a low conversion rate, this might indicate that while people are interested enough to click, they're not following through on the application. This could signal issues with the landing page, application process, or the alignment of ad content with audience expectations.

- **How to Track:** To monitor the conversion rate, you'll need to set up tracking links or pixel codes (such as Facebook Pixel or Google Tag Manager) on your landing page. This is a slightly more complicated metric to track. However, it is incredibly powerful, so I encourage your team to learn this important process. A tracking pixel is a small piece of code embedded into the webpage that records user actions after they click on your ad, like visiting the application form or completing the submission. Start by installing the pixel code on the webpage where the conversion should occur. Then, set up a conversion event in your ad platform's analytics dashboard to track that action. Many platforms, like Facebook and Google Ads, provide step-by-step setup guides and visual tracking reports, making measuring and analyzing conversions easier. Though it requires an initial setup, tracking conversions gives you invaluable data on ad effectiveness and helps identify potential areas for improvement in the recruitment process.

- **Improvement Tips:** To boost conversion rates, ensure that the landing page aligns closely with the content of your advertisement and provides a seamless, user-friendly experience. Use clear, compelling calls to action that guide visitors toward taking the next step and minimize distractions on the page to keep their focus on the intended action. Directing your social media campaign to a dedicated careers page or recruitment section on your website is ideal. This way, potential candidates who click on the ad are immediately taken to the most relevant information, making it easy for them to find exactly what they're interested in and increasing the likelihood of conversion.

8. **Frequency**

- **Description:** Frequency indicates how often a user sees your ad over a specific period. High frequency can signal oversaturation, potentially leading to ad fatigue, where users ignore or even become annoyed by the ad. While it's important for your target audience to see your advertisement multiple times to increase familiarity and brand recognition, there is a fine line between creating awareness and causing viewer fatigue. Striking the right balance ensures that your ad remains effective and engaging without overwhelming viewers, which can help maintain a positive perception of your agency and its message while being cognizant of your budget.

- **How to Track:** Frequency is shown in the performance metrics section of most ad platforms. It's calculated by dividing impressions by reach.

- **Improvement Tips:** Aim to keep frequency moderate, around 2-3 views per user. If frequency becomes high, change the images or video in your campaign or rotate in new messages to prevent ad fatigue. If someone sees the same image and text dozens of times, they will likely ignore it, and your campaign's performance will suffer. Keep a close eye on this metric, especially for ads that have been active for several weeks.

9. **Ad Relevance Score/Quality Score**

- **Description:** This score reflects how relevant your ad is to your target audience. A high relevance or quality score usually means your ad is engaging and well-matched to your audience's interests, which can also help reduce costs. If done correctly, your campaign should target individuals who are highly likely to be interested in a law enforcement career.

- **How to Track:** Relevance scores are available in ad performance metrics on your campaign's page. Low relevance scores may indicate a mismatch between the ad content and the audience.

- **Improvement Tips:** Improve relevance scores by ensuring the ad aligns with your audience's interests. Use feedback from analytics to refine visuals and messages, ensuring each element speaks to the needs and values of the intended audience. As you spend more time with social media advertising, you will quickly learn what content does better or worse with your audience, allowing you to make changes and improve all your metrics.

10. **A/B Testing**

- **Description:** A/B testing involves running two variations of an ad to determine which performs better. It allows you to compare factors like images, headlines, and calls to action to see what resonates most. I recommend that you always start with at least two advertisement versions. This allows you to see which one performs better, allocate more resources to it, and make changes to the advertisement that isn't performing as well. You should consistently review metrics to ensure your advertisements continue to provide the best results.

- **How to Track:** Set up A/B tests within the ad platform to monitor performance differences between ad variations. Most social media platforms will have a section labeled A/B test, making it very easy to set up two ad variations within the same campaign. Be sure to focus on the critical metrics like CTR, CPC, and conversions.

- **Improvement Tips:** Use A/B testing consistently to refine your ads based on data. Testing single elements at a time, such as images or your call-to-action wording. If you change too many parts of the advertisement, you won't be able to determine which change caused the improvement. Start with a low daily budget, allow each ad variation to run for a few days to a week, and continue trying different variations until you find the best version for your organization. Then, you can up the budget and watch the result roll in!

These are some of the most common terms you will see as you begin to utilize social media advertising to bolster your agency's recruiting efforts. Remember, while tracking the metrics of your campaigns is critical, don't let these terms and numbers overwhelm you and cause analysis paralysis. No advertisement will ever be perfect, and you will certainly become better and more comfortable with the process the longer you run these types of advertisements. Start with a small budget, learn the ins and outs of the process, and slowly increase your budget over time as you begin to feel more comfortable and see the results of your efforts.

While all social media platforms have their own advertising options and each has its own benefits, LinkedIn, as the world's largest professional networking platform, offers unmatched potential for reaching candidates with precision. With its robust paid advertising tools, LinkedIn enables agencies to hone in on specific candidate profiles based on criteria like location, education level, field of study, job titles, professional interests, and even membership in certain LinkedIn groups. This powerful targeting capability allows you to design tailored campaigns for different recruiting needs. For example, if it's early in the year and you're looking to engage soon-to-graduate college seniors majoring in criminal justice, political science, or other related fields, you can set parameters to display your ads only to students who are likely exploring their post-graduation career options.

If you're attending a career fair at a university, social media campaigns allow you to strategically target college students in that specific location in the weeks leading up to the event. By creating a campaign tailored to your desired audience, you can notify students of your agency's presence at the fair, highlight the career opportunities you offer, and encourage them to connect with your recruiters at the event. This approach shifts your recruitment efforts from the reactive strategy of simply showing up and hoping for engagement to actively building anticipation and interest among qualified candidates before you even arrive. Such campaigns enhance visibility, position your agency as a proactive, desirable employer, and increase your chances of drawing engaged, interested candidates to your booth. By combining traditional recruitment tactics with modern digital strategies, you create a comprehensive recruitment plan that maximizes your agency's reach, engagement, and overall success in attracting high-quality candidates.

Similarly, if your agency's goal is to attract seasoned law enforcement professionals, LinkedIn allows you to craft a campaign that specifically targets experienced police officers and deputy sheriffs who have indicated that they're open to new career opportunities. This targeted approach helps you connect with candidates who not only meet your agency's qualifications but are also primed for a career change. The precision of LinkedIn's advertising platform significantly enhances the quality of the leads you receive, as it delivers your message directly to those who are most likely to be interested in and qualified for your roles. This saves time, reduces outreach costs, and increases the likelihood of building a pool of candidates who are genuinely engaged and eager to bring their skills to your agency.

As we conclude this important chapter, social media advertising has transformed the recruitment landscape, offering law enforcement agencies unparalleled tools to reach, engage, and attract top-tier talent. Unlike traditional advertising, where messages are shared with broad, sometimes disinterested audiences, social media enables agencies to directly reach individuals who have shown a genuine interest in law enforcement careers or possess relevant skills. By leveraging platforms like Facebook, Instagram, LinkedIn, and X, agencies can ensure that their message lands in front of people most likely to become their future officers, detectives, and public servants. This tailored approach not only saves resources but also enhances the quality of applicants by ensuring that your agency connects with those with the strongest potential to succeed in a law enforcement career.

The power of targeted advertising on social media lies not only in its precision but also in its flexibility. Agencies can start with a modest budget, gather data on campaign performance, and optimize their strategies accordingly. Metrics like cost-per-click, conversion rate, and engagement rate provide valuable insights into ad effectiveness, allowing recruitment teams to adjust their campaigns on the fly. If a specific ad resonates well with a particular demographic, agencies can invest more in that area, boosting engagement and response. This level of control is crucial in a field where every dollar of a recruitment budget counts.

Additionally, social media serves as a gateway to meaningful interactions that extend beyond a simple application submission. When done effectively, agencies can create a sense of connection with potential recruits by highlighting the human side of law enforcement, the teamwork, dedication, and community impact that make a career in this field so rewarding. By sharing authentic stories of service, personal testimonials, and community initiatives, agencies build a narrative that resonates with recruits and inspires them to envision a future with the department. This engagement-driven approach helps to foster long-term interest and trust in the agency.

However, social media advertising does not replace traditional recruitment methods; instead, it enhances them. Combining in-person events, like career fairs and community events, with targeted digital campaigns creates a well-rounded recruitment strategy. Digital ads can build interest before these events, ensuring attendees know about your agency and are excited to connect with recruiters in per-

COLIN WHITTINGTON

son. By integrating both strategies, agencies can expand their reach while retaining the essential personal touch in law enforcement recruitment. This hybrid approach positions agencies as adaptable, forward-thinking employers dedicated to finding the right people to join their organizations.

Looking ahead, social media will continue to evolve, offering law enforcement agencies even more advanced tools for recruiting. Some of the strategies discussed in this chapter may become outdated within just a few years due to the fast-paced nature of digital trends, making it essential for recruitment teams to stay informed and adaptable. I encourage those involved in recruitment to embrace this dynamic environment, staying on top of emerging trends to ensure they're reaching the best talent effectively. While specific methods will change, the need to remain flexible, candidate-centered, and innovative will always be at the core of attracting qualified police officers, deputy sheriffs, and federal agents.

Agencies that take a proactive approach to adopting these evolving strategies will gain a significant advantage in recruiting top talent. By recognizing social media as a powerful, integral component of modern recruitment, law enforcement departments can connect with potential recruits in ways that are not only more meaningful but also cost-effective, maximizing the return on every recruitment dollar spent. Agencies can strengthen their outreach through data-driven, targeted social media strategies, fostering genuine interest and building connections that encourage applicants to envision a future within their ranks.

Moreover, a strong social media presence humanizes the agency, showing recruits a glimpse into the community impact and teamwork that make law enforcement careers so fulfilling. By showcasing real stories, highlighting personal achievements, and sharing moments that resonate with viewers, agencies create a compelling narrative that attracts individuals who share these values and are eager to contribute. This approach draws more applicants who are aligned with the agency's mission, values, and community focus.

As the digital landscape advances, agencies that integrate social media into their core recruitment strategy will set the standard in law enforcement hiring, driving positive outcomes regarding the quality of recruits and public perception. Embracing social media as a flexible and essential tool for outreach empowers agencies to remain competitive in an ever-evolving job market. With a forward-thinking, data-focused approach, law enforcement agencies can meet and even exceed their recruitment goals, building dedicated teams ready to protect and serve with commitment and integrity.

COLIN WHITTINGTON

# CHAPTER SIX
# THE FINER THINGS

The most successful companies in the private sector are constantly innovating their recruiting and hiring practices to attract the top talent in the market. They leverage Applicant Tracking Systems (ATS) to broadcast job openings across multiple job boards and employment sites, creating broad reach and consistent candidate pipelines. These organizations implement clear policies and systems for their recruiters, allowing streamlined, uniform processes across their teams. They actively monitor Key Performance Indicators (KPIs) to measure and refine their efforts, always looking for ways to streamline and improve their processes. And, perhaps most notably, they incentivize and seek employee referrals. By encouraging current employees to bring in candidates, they expand their talent pool and promote a culture of ownership in the hiring process. Law enforcement agencies could benefit from studying these strategies, as adopting even a few of these approaches could significantly strengthen their recruiting capabilities.

In my role as Chief Executive Officer of Recruiting Heroes, I have had the privilege of working with law enforcement agencies across the country to assess and refine their recruiting practices. Many of these departments reach out to us because they are struggling to fill open positions and are frustrated by their seeming inability to attract enough qualified applicants. When my team and I begin working with an agency, we typically start by examining their current pro-

COLIN WHITTINGTON

cesses and asking a series of targeted questions. This initial assessment often reveals underlying procedural and cultural issues significantly contributing to recruitment challenges. Identifying these roadblocks allows us to pinpoint areas for improvement and work with the agency to create more efficient and effective hiring practices.

A common misconception among law enforcement agencies is that improving recruitment requires substantial financial investment. This belief has led many departments to offer hiring bonuses of $20,000 or even $100,000 in a desperate attempt to bolster their recruiting numbers. While I firmly believe that law enforcement officers across the country deserve higher pay for the critical work they perform, these financial incentives often serve as a crutch, masking the deeper issues behind agency vacancy rates. Not only do hiring bonuses risk attracting the wrong type of candidate, but they can also create significant frustration among current employees.

Although hiring bonuses can grab headlines and generate a temporary surge of interest in job openings, they are far from a sustainable solution to the law enforcement recruitment challenges. These large financial incentives can have unintended consequences that undermine an agency's long-term goals. For one, they often attract candidates more motivated by financial gain than a genuine desire to serve in law enforcement. This trend is reflected in most law enforcement job advertisements I've encountered in recent years, which focus almost exclusively on the financial aspects of the job. Headlines scream sign-on bonus amounts or highlight top-end salary ranges while offering little information about the agency, its values, or the realities of the position itself.

While competitive pay is undeniably important, the nature of policing requires individuals who are passionate about their jobs, deeply committed to their communities, and resilient in the face of adversity. When recruiting strategies prioritize financial incentives over all else, agencies risk attracting candidates who lack these critical qualities. This approach not only jeopardizes hiring quality, but it also raises the possibility of future retention and performance issues. After all, how long can a dollar-motivated officer stay in such a demanding, identity-defining profession as law enforcement? True success in this field entails more than just a paycheck. To face the job's unique challenges, you must have a sense of purpose, a commitment to service, and the ability to be resilient.

Moreover, hiring bonuses can breed resentment among existing employees. Officers who have served faithfully for years may feel undervalued when new hires receive lucrative incentives for joining the department. This frustration is often compounded when agencies fail to implement retention-focused strategies, such as career development programs, performance-based raises, or lateral opportunities that reward loyalty and tenure. As discussed in Chapter 2, when morale suffers among seasoned staff, departments risk losing their most experienced and knowledgeable officers, creating a vicious turnover cycle that bonuses alone cannot fix.

Another issue with relying on hiring bonuses is their lack of sustainability. Public service budgets, including those for law enforcement, are often constrained and subject to shifting political priorities. While a department may secure funding for a one-time hiring campaign, maintaining competitive salaries, creating systemized recruiting strategies, providing quality training, and investing in long-term officer success requires consistent, well-planned financial strategy and commitments. Over-reliance on bonuses can drain resources from these essential areas, weakening the department's foundation and functionality.

Ultimately, hiring bonuses should complement, not replace, a broader, holistic recruitment strategy.By addressing the root causes of recruitment struggles, such as outdated policies, lack of technological integration, and insufficient community and departmental engagement, agencies can build resilient teams equipped to serve their communities effectively. The goal is not just to fill vacancies but to cultivate a workforce that is motivated, skilled, and aligned with the department's mission and values.

I believe a fundamental shift in mindset and the prioritization of some key processes are crucial for the success of law enforcement recruiting. For example, using a basic Applicant Tracking System (ATS) enables you to post job openings on multiple job boards simultaneously, centralize applications, create structured processes for your staff to follow, and track Key Performance Indicators (KPIs). This cost-effective tool can significantly broaden your reach and streamline the hiring process. Additionally, establishing a structured referral system that encourages officers and staff to recommend candidates can expand your agency's applicant pool at minimal cost to your department. By tracking how candidates first learn about your agency, you can also identify the most effective recruitment channels, allowing you to focus resources on high-performing areas while removing or working to improve others. Simple yet strategic adjustments like these show that recruitment success relies more on targeted efforts and thoughtful planning than on a large budget.

Throughout this chapter, I will outline how we guide agencies through the process of addressing their vacancy crises by taking a closer look at their strengths and weaknesses. This analysis begins with identifying what works well within the agency's current approach, as building on existing strengths often requires fewer resources and yields quicker results. From there, we address the practices that are holding them back. Whether it's an outdated policy or an inefficient application process, small tweaks can significantly impact an agency's overall recruitment strategy.

It's crucial to recognize that no two agencies are identical, and each has its own unique priorities, budgets, and recruitment needs. Consequently, some strategies that work exceptionally well for one department may not be relevant or feasible for another. I encourage you to approach the information in this chapter with an open mind and consider which insights might be adaptable to your agency's particular context. Sometimes, adopting just one new tactic can produce noticeable improvements without requiring a complete overhaul.

When assessing potential changes, I advise agencies to consider the long-term effects on recruitment and overall departmental culture. Effective recruiting strategies do more than bring in new hires; they help create a supportive and collaborative environment where employees feel invested in the agency's success. Law enforcement agencies that build recruitment into their cultural fabric find it easier to maintain staffing levels and often see higher retention rates. Cultivating a culture that values every member's contribution to recruiting is a key part of sustainable hiring.

As you read this chapter, take a moment to reflect on your agency's policies and hiring practices. Are there inefficiencies that slow down recruitment? Could private-sector strategies help streamline the process? Most importantly, how can you foster a culture where hiring is a shared responsibility that engages both leadership and frontline officers? Every agency, no matter its size or resources, has the potential to improve recruitment and retention. With the proper adjustments, yours can attract top talent, strengthen your workforce, and build a team that is not only more resilient but better equipped to serve your community. Let's get started.

## AN EFFICIENT HIRING PROCESS

Anyone who has been involved in recruiting, background investigations, or the hiring process for a law enforcement agency, especially in recent years, knows the significant challenges it presents. Attracting the right candidate, guiding them through a rigorous selection process, and ultimately securing their commitment is a complex and often unpredictable journey. Every step must align seamlessly to ensure the candidate is not only qualified for the job but also the right fit for the agency and the profession. Agencies must do more than identify interested applicants; they must navigate extensive background checks, offer competitive salaries, and keep candidates engaged through a demanding hiring process. One misstep in communication, expectations, or timing can mean the difference between hiring a promising recruit and losing them to another opportunity.

COLIN WHITTINGTON

Simply getting individuals to apply can seem like an insurmountable hurdle for many agencies. The profession faces unique demands and scrutiny, which can deter prospective candidates from ever considering a career in law enforcement. The national media and outspoken politicians do little to improve these challenges. The challenges are far from over for those few candidates who do apply. The background investigation process is often lengthy and thorough, and many applicants are lost along the way. Some are disqualified due to an issue in their background, while others withdraw from the process, often discouraged by the prolonged timeline or accepting an offer with another organization.

Given these hurdles, law enforcement agencies must take every possible step to streamline and enhance their hiring processes. By focusing on the elements they can control, agencies can minimize potential issues and create a more efficient and effective pathway from recruitment to hiring. Law enforcement agencies around the country are all competing for a small and ever-shrinking pool of interested and suitable candidates. In this increasingly competitive landscape, small adjustments to the hiring process are not just beneficial; they are essential for attracting and retaining the dedicated professionals each department needs to fill vacancies and maintain public order.

Now, I am not suggesting that law enforcement agencies lower their standards or cut corners in the background investigation process. On the contrary, the stakes are too high to compromise on quality. Law enforcement is an essential pillar of our society, and we owe it to our communities to ensure that only the most qualified, principled, caring, and capable individuals serve as police officers, deputy sheriffs, correctional officers, and federal agents. The demands and responsibilities of these roles require individuals with exceptional integrity, resilience, and commitment to justice. These are not qualities that should ever be sacrificed for speed.

That said, efficiency in the background investigation process is not only desirable but necessary. A lengthy, drawn-out investigation can cause promising candidates to lose interest or accept positions elsewhere, especially in today's competitive job market. Every delay risks the loss of individuals who might otherwise be excellent additions to the agency. But efficiency doesn't mean compromise. By adopting best practices, leveraging technology, and prioritizing clear, streamlined workflows, agencies can enhance their background investigations' efficiency without sacrificing quality. When done correctly, these tools and strategies can significantly improve the effectiveness and efficiencies of your background investigation process.

## SPREAD THE WORD

As discussed in Chapter 5, one of the most common challenges I see law enforcement agencies face is their overreliance on a single platform to advertise job openings. For most departments, this is a city or county website, not even their own. This limited approach is a critical mistake, likely costing these agencies hundreds of potential applicants. While it's true that an official town, city, county, or federal application is a necessary part of the hiring process, this requirement shouldn't deter agencies from actively promoting their job opportunities across multiple channels.

Relying solely on an official government website severely limits the reach of your job openings. This approach assumes that potential candidates already know about your agency, understand its mission, and are actively seeking out your opportunities. It creates a multi-step hurdle: candidates must first hear about your department, recognize its value, and then proactively search for job postings on a specific government site. For many talented individuals, this process might never begin simply because they're unaware your agency exists, that you are hiring, or where to go to apply for your open positions.

Relying on a single platform means your agency must work incredibly hard for every application it receives. With this limited approach, nearly all applicants will come from your team's proactive advertising and outreach efforts, with very few candidates finding your department organically. This creates an unnecessarily heavy burden on your recruiting team, as they must constantly push the message rather than letting the job announcement work for them.

By contrast, casting a wider net through multiple platforms and websites allows your job postings to reach a much larger audience. When your job opportunities are visible on dozens of career-focused websites, social media platforms, and industry-specific boards, you're not just relying on direct outreach. You're also benefiting from the natural spread of information. This strategy enables passive job seekers, who may not actively search government websites but are open to new opportunities, to find your agency and discover the opportunities you offer.

Combining your agency's proactive outreach with a wide distribution of your job announcement creates a steady flow of applications from a diverse and qualified pool of candidates. You significantly broaden your reach by leveraging multiple platforms and communication channels, ensuring individuals from various backgrounds, experiences, and communities see your job opportunities. This approach lightens the workload for your recruiting team, freeing them to focus on engaging with the most promising candidates, and increases your chances of attracting talented individuals who may never have considered a career in law enforcement if they had not encountered your job announcement. A well-strategized distribution plan ensures your agency stands out in a competitive job market, helping you secure the best possible talent to serve your community effectively.

One of the most impactful ways law enforcement agencies can expand their reach is by leveraging job boards to share their career openings. Platforms like LinkedIn, Indeed, Glassdoor, and even industry-specific sites like Police1 have become invaluable tools for connecting with a diverse pool of potential candidates. These platforms are where modern job seekers are actively searching for their next opportunities, making them a critical component of any successful recruitment strategy.

LinkedIn is an especially powerful resource for reaching professionals seeking their next career. With its ability to target candidates based on location, skills, and interests, LinkedIn allows agencies to be strategic about who sees their job postings. Military veterans, who are often drawn to careers in law enforcement after their years of military service, can often be found on LinkedIn. Websites like Indeed and Glassdoor receive tens of thousands of visitors daily from candidates all over America, many of whom are just starting on their professional journeys.

These candidates can easily be convinced of the incredible potential of a career in law enforcement. Sharing your job openings on these platforms will drastically increase your application numbers, giving you a greater selection of which candidates to consider for your department.

## APPLICANT TRACKING SYSTEMS

Managing multiple job postings across numerous platforms might initially seem daunting and overwhelming, but applicant tracking systems (ATS) provide a cost-effective and efficient solution that simplifies the process. ATS software has become a staple in the private sector and is used by organizations of all sizes to streamline recruitment efforts. These systems allow agencies to create job postings in one centralized location, automatically distribute them to dozens of job boards, and manage all applications from one centralized hub.

At Recruiting Heroes, we rely on an ATS that partners with over 35 career-focused websites. When my team creates a job announcement, it is instantly shared across all those platforms, vastly expanding our reach without my team having to create accounts and monitor each website individually. As candidates apply on these job boards, their applications and resumes are seamlessly funneled back to our ATS, where we can review the applications, message the candidates, and create an organization system from one user-friendly dashboard. This centralized approach eliminates the need to juggle multiple accounts or manually track applications, freeing up valuable time to focus on what matters most: engaging with and selecting the best candidates.

Another significant advantage of using an ATS is the ability to monitor and analyze the performance of job postings across various platforms. Metrics such as the number of views, applications submitted, and candidate demographics provide valuable insights into which platforms are most effective at driving results. For example, your team might discover that your police officer job announcement is performing exceptionally well on Indeed. This success could prompt you to explore paid advertisements on that platform, further amplifying your reach and maximizing application rates. On the other hand, you might notice less engagement on LinkedIn, leading you to revisit the wording of your post to better highlight the key benefits and unique aspects of the position.

This data-driven approach empowers agencies to refine their recruitment strategies, ensuring that time and resources are directed toward the methods that actually work. By identifying trends and pinpointing opportunities for improvement, your team can continually optimize job postings to attract a higher volume of quality applicants. This level of insight is invaluable for law enforcement agencies operating on tight recruiting budgets. It enables you to allocate funds strategically, focusing on efforts that yield the greatest return in terms of applications and successful hires. In today's competitive job market, leveraging data to guide your recruiting decisions is essential for staying ahead and continuously working to improve your recruiting and hiring efforts.

Unlike clunky government websites that have very little experience in recruiting, ATS software works with dozens of career-focused websites that strive to create an easy and enjoyable experience for their users. This means that your job announcements are more visible to your department's candidates and make the actual application process significantly more seamless and straightforward. In an age where law enforcement agencies must fight for every application they receive, the worst thing that can happen is for an interested candidate to walk away from an application due to a complicated and hard-to-use system.

So far, ATS has yet to gain widespread adoption within the law enforcement profession. As discussed earlier in this book, the profession has a long history of being slow to embrace change, often clinging to traditional practices that no longer meet the demands of the modern recruiting landscape. This resistance to innovation is particularly evident in the belief held by many departments that candidates must apply exclusively through the official government website. While this approach fulfills certain procedural requirements, it severely limits agencies from tapping into the vast and ever-expanding digital world of recruitment tools and resources.

By relying solely on government websites, departments miss out on the significant advantages ATS platforms can provide. These systems are designed to streamline and optimize every stage of the recruitment process, from advertising job postings across multiple platforms to tracking applicants and managing communications in one centralized hub. Without an ATS, law enforcement agencies create unnecessary bottlenecks for their internal teams and fail to meet candidates where they are: on career websites, social media platforms, and mobile applications.

Adopting an applicant tracking system does not mean bypassing or disregarding official application processes. Agencies can use an ATS to enhance their recruitment efforts by attracting candidates through popular job boards and digital platforms, ensuring a broader and more diverse pool of applicants. Once candidates express interest, the ATS can serve as a bridge, allowing background investigators or recruiters to establish personal connections with those candidates. Through these interactions, agencies can guide applicants through the official steps, including applying on the government website to ensure compliance with established protocols.

This dual approach respects the necessary formalities of government hiring processes and humanizes the experience for candidates. By leveraging an ATS to create a seamless and supportive journey, agencies demonstrate a commitment to accessibility and engagement. Building these relationships early in the process encourages candidates to remain invested, even during the more rigorous and time-intensive stages of background investigations. This combination of technology and personal connection strengthens the candidate's experience, making applicants more likely to stay committed and successfully complete the process. The days of treating candidates like a number are well behind us. Agencies must learn to have a hands-on and personalized approach to hiring or risk falling behind other departments.

Not only are applicant tracking systems an excellent resource to enhance your department's recruitment efforts, but they can also be surprisingly affordable. Many ATS platforms offer scalable pricing models, allowing agencies to choose a plan that fits their budget and needs. For smaller departments with limited resources, entry-level plans can provide access to essential tools like multi-platform job postings, candidate tracking, and communication management without breaking the bank. Larger agencies, on the other hand, can opt for more comprehensive packages that include advanced analytics, automated workflows, and integrations with existing systems. However, even the more advanced options are still quite reasonably priced. My company's applicant tracking system only costs us $40 per month per user. A very minimal cost for the fantastic service it provides. It streamlines our hiring processes and takes out a significant number of administrative duties, allowing my team to focus on more critical tasks. In the long run, ATS can significantly reduce recruitment expenses by helping agencies attract more qualified candidates faster and retain them through an efficient, professional process.

The digital age has revolutionized the job search process, with candidates now expecting application experiences that are user-friendly, accessible, and efficient. Unfortunately, many law enforcement

COLIN WHITTINGTON

agencies remain tied to outdated systems that frustrate applicants and deter highly qualified individuals from pursuing opportunities. Applicant tracking systems provide a powerful solution, bridging the gap between traditional hiring practices and the modern expectations of today's workforce. By leveraging an ATS, agencies can expand their reach, streamline their recruitment efforts, and meet candidates where they are, all while maintaining adherence to official hiring protocols. If your agency is serious about improving recruitment and attracting top talent, I strongly encourage you to explore how an ATS can transform your approach and enhance your results.

## OPTIMIZING YOUR APPLICATION

One of the simplest yet most impactful steps law enforcement agencies can take to improve recruitment is optimizing their application flow. A streamlined application process can prevent unnecessary candidate drop-offs and encourage more applicants to complete it. In today's competitive job market, a complex or outdated application can deter qualified candidates who may have multiple offers on the table or who expect a quick, straightforward hiring experience.

The younger generations are used to a digital world that moves at lightning speed. They expect mobile-friendly, intuitive interactions for virtually everything they do, from ordering food to applying for jobs. For many young applicants, an outdated, cumbersome application process is more than just a hassle; it can be a dealbreaker that dissuades them from considering a career with your department. Today's candidates want the convenience of completing tasks quickly and seamlessly on their mobile devices without the added steps of printing, handwriting, scanning, or mailing forms.

Yet, many law enforcement agencies still rely on outdated, paper-based application systems. In my work with departments across the country, I frequently encounter application processes that require candidates to print forms, fill them out by hand, and deliver them in person or by mail. Imagine a candidate who is deciding which departments to apply to. With some agencies, he finds a fast, efficient digital application process that takes minutes to complete. But to apply to your department, he would need to find a place to print the application (most Gen Zers do not own printers), write out answers by hand (an increasingly rare skill for many of today's young adults), and mail it back (something many Gen Zers have never had to do). Faced with these hurdles, what are the chances he'll choose your department over others with a simple digital application? Slim to none. He will move on to a department that offers a faster and more modern application experience.

Even agencies that have adopted digital applications often fall short of providing a truly user-friendly experience. Many systems lack mobile optimization, requiring candidates to use a computer or laptop to apply. This creates a significant barrier for individuals who primarily rely on phones or tablets and may only have limited access to a computer in work or educational settings. Failing to accommodate these candidates is a critical oversight that can significantly reduce your pool of candidates simply because they cannot complete the application process.

At the Loudoun County Sheriff's Office, we tackled this issue by ensuring our application was fully accessible on any device, allowing candidates to choose how they wanted to apply. Our recruiting team collaborated with the technology division to create a system that was easy to access and intuitive to use. Modernizing and streamlining the application process is crucial for law enforcement agencies to attract younger, tech-savvy applicants. This includes offering mobile-compatible digital applications with clear instructions, responsive layouts, and fast load times. While this may seem obvious for agencies already using digital systems, it's surprising how many departments have yet to implement these changes. If your agency is one of them, making the digitalization and accessibility of your application process a top priority is essential.

COLIN WHITTINGTON

## CONTINUOUSLY MOVING FORWARD

The background investigation process is a lengthy and often exhausting journey for candidates aspiring to join the law enforcement profession. Agencies frequently require applicants to complete an array of steps, including physical fitness tests, panel interviews, polygraphs, background interviews, medical and psychological evaluations, and more. For those unfamiliar with the intricate process, it can feel like an unending series of hurdles. Decades ago, the rigidity and impersonal nature of these investigations were considered standard practice, with candidates often treated as little more than a number, one among hundreds or even thousands. However, in today's climate of widespread vacancies in law enforcement, clinging to these outdated models can significantly damage your agency's ability to address your vacancy problems.

Candidates are now evaluating agencies just as much as agencies are evaluating them. While it's reasonable to expect candidates to demonstrate commitment and perseverance during the hiring process, it's equally important for recruiting teams to acknowledge and adapt to evolving cultural and generational expectations. Modern candidates value transparency and consistent communication throughout the hiring process. They want to feel they're progressing steadily toward their goal of becoming a law enforcement officer. Gone are the days when departments could rely on an overflow of highly motivated, qualified applicants to fill positions. Today, departments must proactively ensure the hiring experience is engaging, informative, and reflects their need to attract top-tier talent.

Far too often, I've seen agencies neglect the crucial first step of making meaningful contact with candidates upon receiving their applications. Candidates tell me all the time about receiving only a generic "thank you for applying" email or, even worse, no confirmation or acknowledgment at all. Some candidates wait weeks or even months without receiving any follow-up from recruiters or background investigators. Surprisingly, even certified officers with prior law enforcement experience have shared similarly frustrating

COLIN WHITTINGTON

delayed responses from agencies they have applied to. These candidates were not applying to agencies with full staffing but those who were advertising significant hiring bonuses in an apparent push to address urgent staffing shortages.

This raises a critical question: how can an agency struggling with vacancies afford to overlook the importance of creating a strong first impression or building immediate relationships with those hoping to become law enforcement officers with their department? Failing to engage candidates promptly sends an unintended message that the department is disorganized or indifferent to their interests. This perception can drive potential recruits to pursue opportunities with other agencies that demonstrate a stronger commitment to building relationships early in the process. A timely, personalized response acknowledges the candidate's application and sets the tone for the professional, welcoming, and supportive experience they should expect throughout their journey with your department.

An organization's success is directly tied to the efficiency and effectiveness of its processes and systems. By systemizing your recruiting and background investigation process, you not only enhance operational efficiency but also significantly improve the candidate's experience. Begin by setting clear standards for initial communication. Ideally, your agency should contact candidates within two business days of receiving their application. This prompt response sets a positive tone, demonstrating that your agency values the candidate's interest and is committed to a professional and transparent process from the outset.

In this initial message, thank the candidate for applying and provide a clear overview of what they can expect during the hiring and background investigation process. While you don't need to schedule every appointment immediately, offering an honest and transparent summary of the steps ahead will set clear expectations and reduce uncertainty on behalf of the candidate. Include details about the key components of the process, the estimated timeline, and a Frequently Asked Questions (FAQ) document addressing common concerns.

This proactive communication empowers candidates to prepare for the journey ahead and minimizes the number of routine questions your staff may receive in the coming weeks.

Once the initial contact has been made, promptly schedule the candidate for their first assessment, whether a physical fitness test, panel interview, or other initial step in your background investigation process. Ideally, this should occur within two to four weeks of their application submission. A swift start reduces the risk of losing qualified candidates to other agencies and maintains their momentum and enthusiasm. Chances are good that the candidate applied to other agencies around the same time she applied to yours. Every day counts!

One effective strategy for streamlining the recruitment process is hosting regular, consistent group assessment events. At my agency, we implemented monthly Physical Abilities Assessments (PAA). All qualified candidates who had applied within the previous month were invited to complete our physical abilities test and participate in a panel interview. Before the event, we required candidates to complete a digital screening questionnaire as part of their application. Our background investigators carefully reviewed the candidates' answers to these questions, allowing us to identify and remove candidates who had disclosed disqualifying information about their background from consideration. This pre-screening step ensured that only eligible candidates were invited to the assessment event, saving time and resources while maintaining the integrity of the selection process.

This monthly schedule provided several benefits. First, it ensured no candidate had to wait more than a few weeks to begin the process, keeping them engaged and motivated. Second, it allowed us to complete two important parts of the background process for a large group of candidates simultaneously, maximizing staff resources and creating a structured, repeatable process. By systemizing the early stages of recruitment, your agency can maintain a steady pipeline of candidates, reduce delays, and foster a sense of organization and professionalism that reflects positively on your department.

Upon finishing the initial group assessments, I urge you to keep the momentum going. Have your recruiting and background investigation teams review the results from the event on their next duty day to decide which candidates meet or exceed standards and which do not. Reach out to candidates within two business days of the event, letting them know if they have been removed from consideration or if they will continue in the hiring process. Not only is this practice respectful to the candidates, but it also minimizes the risk that you will lose applicants who feel they aren't progressing through the hiring process in a timely manner. Agencies are often slow in communication, leading to frustration and dropouts from competitive applicants. Don't let that be an issue with your department.

Assign each candidate to a dedicated background investigator to streamline the process and enhance the applicant's experience. Unlike the fragmented approach that often arises when multiple investigators are involved, a single point of contact minimizes confusion and ensures clear communication. This allows the investigator to build rapport with the applicant, creating a more personalized and professional interaction. The assigned investigator should prioritize maintaining consistent communication, promptly scheduling necessary appointments, and providing the applicant with a clear understanding of the expected timeline. Moreover, this investigator becomes a continuous resource, guiding the candidate and addressing any concerns arising throughout the background investigation process. This approach fosters trust and reinforces the agency's commitment to the applicant's success.

To further enhance the candidate experience, investigators should send weekly emails to their assigned candidates. These communications need not be lengthy but should keep the applicant informed and engaged. For instance, an email might confirm an upcoming appointment, request additional documentation, or check in to see if the candidate has any questions or concerns. Such proactive outreach demonstrates that the agency values applicants and views them as individuals, not just faceless numbers in a bureaucratic process. This thoughtful approach is fundamental given the historical challenges many candidates faced when entering the law enforcement field in the late 20th and early 21st centuries. Back then, candidates often felt overlooked or undervalued, leading to frustration and sometimes disillusionment. By contrast, modern agencies adopting a personalized communication strategy set themselves apart as forward-thinking organizations genuinely caring about the people they aim to recruit. This human touch enhances the applicant's experience and reflects positively on the agency's culture and professionalism.

## ANALYZE THE DATA

Law enforcement agencies should constantly analyze their hiring practices to identify areas that can be improved and made more efficient. Reducing delays in the recruitment process starts with understanding where things tend to slow down. Every agency has its pain points and bottlenecks. Background checks that seem to go on forever, interviews delayed by scheduling conflicts, polygraph examiner availability, or candidates waiting weeks for simple updates. These bottlenecks can cause frustration and result in the agency losing some of its best candidates. Top talent doesn't wait forever. When communication is lacking, applicants may assume the worst and move on to other opportunities with different departments. The key to preventing this lies in constant self-assessment. By regularly reviewing the process and pinpointing common delays, agencies can uncover what's holding them back and begin to make meaningful changes.

Sometimes, the solution isn't about speeding up the process but improving how it's communicated. Delays feel longer when candidates are left in the dark. Clear communication can transform an otherwise frustrating wait into a manageable part of the process. Candidates who know where they stand and what comes next are far less likely to disengage. Something as simple as a quick update, an email confirming a scheduled interview or a note explaining that their background check is still in progress can make all the difference. This sense of transparency and respect goes a long way in keeping candidates invested.

Background investigations are the biggest hurdle for many agencies in increasing their hiring numbers. They're necessary, of course, but they don't have to be slow. With the right tools and systems, these checks can be thorough and efficient. Digital platforms that automate parts of the process or standardized checklists for investigators can streamline and systemize the process, eliminating unnecessary delays. When each step is clearly defined and the workload is shared evenly, the entire process flows more smoothly. It's not just about working faster but working smarter, ensuring that every task adds value without adding time. Utilizing data from key performance indicators to improve the efficiency of your background investigation process is critical.

Key Performance Indicators (KPIs) are measurable benchmarks that organizations use to evaluate the effectiveness and efficiency of specific processes, making them invaluable for law enforcement agencies working to optimize their hiring practices. KPIs provide actionable insights by quantifying performance in key areas, allowing agencies to identify strengths, weaknesses, and opportunities for improvement. One of the most crucial KPIs is time-to-hire, which tracks the total duration of the recruitment process from the moment a candidate applies to the acceptance of a final job offer. In today's competitive job market, extended hiring timelines can deter top-tier talent, often driving highly skilled candidates to seek opportunities with other departments or in entirely different professions. By tracking time-to-hire, departments can identify bottlenecks in their recruitment process, such as lengthy background investigations, delays in interview scheduling, lack of availability for psychological and medical exams, and scheduling challenges for polygraph tests. Addressing these critical issues through targeted solutions enhances the overall efficiency of the hiring process. It ensures that departments remain competitive in attracting and securing top-tier candidates before losing them to other opportunities.

Breaking down time-to-hire into specific stages, such as the time from application submission to initial contact, application to the first assessment, or interview scheduling to completion, can reveal the root causes of delays. For example, as highlighted earlier in this chapter, promptly acknowledging a candidate's application is crucial. It sets a professional tone and helps maintain candidate engagement from the beginning. Even a simple improvement, like measuring and reducing the time it takes for background investigators to make initial contact with candidates, can substantially impact the agency's overall hiring performance. Tracking these aspects of time-to-hire ensures no step is overlooked, paving the way for a smoother, more efficient process.

Another crucial KPI is the candidate drop-off rate, which measures the percentage of applicants who leave the hiring process before completion. These would be candidates who voluntarily withdraw from your hiring process, not those disqualified during the background investigation. High drop-off rates often signal underlying issues like poor communication, prolonged delays, or overly complex procedures. Candidates are more likely to withdraw during lengthy background investigations or after experiencing a lack of timely feedback. Identifying these pain points enables agencies to refine their processes and ensure candidates remain engaged. Simple fixes, such as providing regular updates or setting clear expectations on what they can expect during the background process, can dramatically reduce candidate attrition.

To determine the number of applications your recruiters should aim to generate each year, it's essential to track your hiring conversion rates. This KPI measures the percentage of candidates who successfully progress from application to hire. To calculate your hiring conversion rate, divide the number of officers hired in a year by the total number of applications received, then multiply that by 100. The result will give you the percentage of applicants hired by your agency. For many law enforcement agencies, the hiring conversion rate typically falls between 5% and 10%. This means that for every 100 applications received, only 5 to 10 candidates are approved for hire. Understanding this rate allows you to set realistic recruitment goals and better allocate resources, as we will discuss shortly.

The background investigation completion rate highlights inefficiencies and ensures this critical portion of the hiring process is thorough and timely. While every background investigation is unique, establishing standardized workflows and processes can not only reduce errors and delays but can also help your team create an optimal completion timeline. Supervisors will then be able to measure metrics such as the percentage of investigations completed within the timeline. When these systems function optimally, the hiring process becomes more seamless, ensuring that high-quality candidates aren't lost to preventable delays.

Effective communication is another area where KPIs can drive improvement. Tracking candidate communication effectiveness ensures applicants feel informed and valued throughout the process. Candidates who receive timely updates, I suggest a minimum weekly email check-in, are far less likely to become disgruntled and withdraw from the process. Agencies can also gather feedback directly from applicants to measure satisfaction and identify areas where communication may fall short. Create a survey for candidates to complete requesting honest feedback on the recruiting and background investigation process, what things went well, and where the agency could improve. Communication should be one of the most critical questions you inquire about in this survey.

In addition to examining the process itself, agencies must consider the workload of individual investigators. KPIs such as investigator productivity metrics help highlight caseload disparities and identify whether additional training or resources are necessary. Monitoring how long investigators spend on each case, their average caseload, and their success rates in completing investigations can help balance workloads and improve efficiency. While in my agency's Employment Services Section, I quickly discovered that I had investigators completing most of the investigations while others took significantly longer and worked far fewer cases. Tracking investigator productivity metrics allowed me to realize this disparity and to quickly find solutions to improve the output of the underperforming investigators.

Measuring investigator productivity within your background investigation team allows you to set realistic expectations about how many new officers you can hire each year. For instance, if your data shows that each investigator completes an average of 30 background investigations a year, and 50% of those investigations result in a hire, you can estimate that each investigator will bring on approximately 15 officers annually. With a team of five investigators, this translates to approximately 75 hires per year. While actual numbers may vary slightly from year to year, this KPI provides a reliable baseline for strategic planning.

KPIs transform hiring from a guessing game into a precise, data-driven process when consistently tracked and analyzed. Begin by identifying the number of officers your agency needs to meet its goals, then work backward to calculate the required volume of applications and investigations to achieve that target. If hiring output needs to increase, you can make informed, actionable decisions grounded in data rather than intuition or guesswork. Options might include allocating additional resources to expand your recruitment or investigative teams, optimizing the hiring process to reduce time-to-hire, enhancing investigator productivity, or improving hiring conversion rates. These strategic adjustments enable your agency to efficiently handle more cases annually and stay competitive in attracting top talent.

Establishing measurable benchmarks, like reducing time-to-hire by 20% or increasing investigator productivity by 10%, transforms vague aspirations into tangible progress. Too often, agencies aim to improve hiring practices without clearly defining success metrics or creating actionable plans. By setting achievable objectives and fine-tuning your systems, your efforts will translate into hiring more qualified officers in less time. The ultimate goal is to design an efficient, transparent, repeatable recruitment process that appeals to top-tier candidates. With data-driven strategies and the right tools, law enforcement agencies can make significant strides in building stronger, more capable teams while better serving their communities.

Tracking and analyzing KPIs may seem daunting, but today's technology has made it simpler and more effective than ever. Software platforms like NEOGOV and Guardian Alliance Technologies offer comprehensive solutions to streamline background investigations and recruitment workflows. These tools automate routine tasks such as jurisdictional checks, maintain centralized records, provide real-time updates on candidate progress, and track key KPIs. Supervisors gain visibility into the process, while investigators can focus on higher-value activities rather than paperwork.

These solutions are often reasonably priced, making them accessible even to smaller agencies. With user-friendly interfaces, they empower departments to monitor metrics such as time-to-hire, candidate drop-off rates, and investigator productivity, allowing for precise identification of bottlenecks and the creation of targeted improvements. These platforms can help create systems for your background investigation process, ensuring that they are efficient and thorough. Outdated methods like paper files or Excel spreadsheets are no longer necessary in a modern recruitment environment.

Investing in the right tools and adopting a metric-driven approach enhances efficiency and makes your agency more attractive to top candidates. A streamlined hiring process reduces turnover, builds stronger teams, and improves community service. Law enforcement agencies can create a transparent, repeatable, and competitive recruitment process by embracing innovation and committing to continuous improvement. This foundation positions your department for sustained success in hiring the best and brightest candidates.

# CHAPTER SEVEN
# RECRUITING IS A TEAM SPORT

During a time of unprecedented challenges in the law enforcement profession, one of the most important realizations agencies must embrace is that a successful recruiting strategy cannot rest solely on the shoulders of recruiting and background investigation teams. Recruitment must become an agency-wide effort to overcome the vacancy crisis that has shaken our profession. From the newest rookie officer to the chief of police, sheriff, or other law enforcement executive, every department member must serve as an official or unofficial recruiter and agency ambassador.

This mindset requires a cultural shift. Agencies must emphasize that recruitment is not just a department within the organization but a shared mission involving every member and every interaction, both professional and personal. Each conversation with a community member, every interaction with a student during a school visit, and even how officers carry themselves during routine patrols contribute to the perception of the agency as a workplace and a partner in public safety.

Building a recruitment culture starts at the top, with leadership setting the tone for the entire agency. Leaders must consistently model behaviors that reflect the values, integrity, and professionalism they expect from their teams. When officers witness their leaders actively advocating for the agency, not just during formal recruiting events but also in everyday interactions, it reinforces the importance of being proud ambassadors of your department's badge. Chiefs and sheriffs who are approachable, visible in their communities, and willing to engage directly with potential recruits send a powerful message that the agency values its people and deeply believes in its mission.

To amplify this impact, consider hosting virtual Q&A sessions where your chief or sheriff personally answers questions from interested candidates, fostering transparency and a direct line of communication. Invite senior leadership to attend recruiting events or physical ability assessments to engage with applicants face-to-face, demonstrating a hands-on commitment to the hiring process. This level of involvement from senior leaders strengthens recruitment efforts and boosts morale within the department. Vacancies place additional burdens on current staff, creating dissatisfaction and morale issues. By being actively involved in recruiting, leadership shows that it is a priority for them, underscoring the importance of adopting a "recruiting as a team" strategy.

When speaking to law enforcement leadership, I always emphasize a simple truth: no one understands what it takes to be an officer in your agency better than the officers currently wearing your uniform and serving your community. These men and women are on the front lines every day, responding to calls for service, using your agency's vehicles and equipment, and experiencing firsthand the benefits and opportunities of being part of your department. Who could possibly be better equipped or positioned to communicate these realities to potential candidates?

Regardless of your department's size, you likely have dozens, hundreds, or even thousands of officers who can serve as unofficial recruiters. This is an untapped resource with incredible potential that so many law enforcement agencies completely overlook. Agencies often place the entire recruiting burden on a handful of recruiters and background investigators, failing to understand that recruiting is a team sport. A truly successful recruiting strategy requires every member of the agency. By equipping your officers with the right information, empowering them with tools and resources, and motivating them with a shared sense of purpose, you can transform your entire team into a dynamic recruiting force. These officers can offer an authentic perspective that resonates far more deeply with potential recruits than any marketing campaign ever could.

Encourage your recruiting teams to hold regular roll call trainings with the various divisions within your agency. I made it a habit to visit deputies and units throughout our agency to discuss recruiting efforts and how they could help bring the best candidates to our department. I gave them resources to answer the most common questions candidates ask during the hiring process, highlighted significant benefits they could share with interested individuals, and taught them where to direct applicants to ensure the candidate could quickly begin the application process.

These presentations, though time-consuming, made a significant impact by encouraging staff to play an active role in recruiting efforts. By presenting information about your hiring processes and emphasizing the importance of bringing candidates to the agency, you can inspire many officers to take a more active role and equip them with the knowledge and resources to assist effectively.

To further help our officers become fantastic unofficial recruiters, we worked with our leadership team to implement small but impactful changes to policies and equipment. First, we created a recruitment incentive for our staff. Any employee, sworn or civilian, who recruited a candidate successfully hired by the agency received a $1,000 reward added to their next paycheck. You can imagine how quickly our recruiting team began receiving high-quality referrals from our coworkers! To ensure employees understand the importance of recommending only strong candidates, make the incentive contingent on the employee completing a reference questionnaire and interview during the applicant's background investigation process.

If financial rewards are not feasible for your department, consider alternative incentives, such as additional vacation days or annual recognition events for employees who help recruit. Be creative. Find alternative solutions that are feasible for your agency and motivating for your team. You'll be amazed at how even small incentives can increase engagement and recruitment efforts.

During my time in employment services, I found that employees rarely recommend candidates they believe would be poor fits for the department. Since their names are tied to their referrals, they are motivated to recommend only high-quality candidates. Many candidates who came to us through our employee referral program were incredibly successful and high-performing deputy sheriffs. Providing even modest incentives can significantly increase this valuable source of candidates many agencies fail to tap into.

Furthermore, an employee referral program empowers your current staff by giving them a tangible role in addressing the agency's hiring challenges. This sense of involvement fosters a deeper connection to the organization's mission. Incentives, whether financial rewards, extra time off, or public recognition, can further enhance morale, creating a win-win situation. Not only does your agency attract quality candidates, but your current team will also feel valued and engaged, leading to improved retention rates.

My team and I developed recruiting-themed business cards, brochures, and cruiser decals to support our deputies in identifying and attracting candidates to our department. These materials featured our recruiting website, starting salary range, and key benefits. The business cards included a designated space for deputies to write their names, giving interested candidates a personal point of reference when applying. This simple yet effective tool streamlined the application process and fostered a stronger connection between applicants and our agency. Over time, we observed many deputies taking the initiative to engage with citizens about job opportunities. Their efforts were recognized through commendations and financial rewards, creating a ripple effect that motivated others to actively contribute to bringing talented individuals onto our team.

Placing your recruiting website on department cruisers is another simple, cost-effective way to increase awareness. Police vehicles naturally draw attention in the community as everyone's head turns when they see a cruiser. Use this visibility to direct citizens to your careers page. Instead of spending thousands of dollars on a stationary billboard on a highway, you can have dozens or hundreds of mobile "billboards" all around your region for just a few hundred dollars. Not all recruiting initiatives have to be expensive.

These are just some of the many ways to involve your entire agency in recruitment and hiring. Be creative and continuously think of new and unique ways to engage your employees in the recruiting process. Whether you are the chief of police or a rookie patrol officer, every member of an agency can and should play a vital role in ensuring the future success of a department by continuously seeking out and recruiting fantastic candidates for sworn law enforcement positions.

## RECRUITING THROUGH COMMUNITY POLICING

Community engagement is a cornerstone of effective law enforcement recruitment, bridging agencies and the local populations they aim to protect. By becoming visible, approachable, and involved in the community, agencies can establish a foundation of trust essential for recruiting the next generation of officers. This trust fosters a positive perception of law enforcement and encourages residents to consider policing as a career. Active participation in community events, outreach programs, and collaborations with local organizations not only highlights the human side of policing but also demystifies the profession. For many, law enforcement may seem inaccessible or misunderstood; community engagement breaks down these barriers.

Participating in local events is one of the most impactful ways to engage with the community and inspire potential recruits. When law

COLIN WHITTINGTON

enforcement officers show up at festivals, charity runs, and neighborhood gatherings, they offer a unique opportunity for the public to interact with them in a setting not tied to enforcement. These informal moments humanize officers, allowing people to see them as approachable and relatable individuals, not just authority figures. These interactions can be transformative for younger generations, especially those from underrepresented communities. Witnessing officers making a positive impact firsthand can spark an interest in law enforcement careers and plant the seeds for future recruits.

My team embraced every opportunity to engage with the community by being highly visible and active participants in a variety of events. Whether it was a small gathering or a large-scale event, we made it our mission to have our recruiting team members present at gatherings across our county and the surrounding region. We proudly drove our agency's recruiting cruiser in every parade, set up recruiting booths at community events, and even went the extra mile, literally. I once ran a 5K race wearing my full uniform, sparking conversations and leaving a lasting impression on other participants and spectators. Through these efforts, we aimed to build strong relationships and foster trust in our community. They also became an integral part of our long-term recruiting strategy.

Recruiting is not an occasional task but a continuous process. It requires getting into the community, highlighting what your agency has to offer, and showing potential candidates why a career in law enforcement is a compelling and meaningful choice. Studies reveal that consumers typically need to see, hear, or engage with a product or service seven or eight times before deciding to act. Companies understand this and craft advertising strategies to ensure their brand stays at the top of their audience's mind. Similarly, law enforcement agencies must consistently promote their opportunities to potential recruits.

A candidate may need to see one of your social media posts, observe your cruiser in a parade, and speak with a recruiter at a career event before she decides to apply to your agency. Each touchpoint plays a role in moving them closer to applying. It's up to you to ensure your agency remains visible, accessible, and consistently present in the community because recruiting isn't just about filling positions. It's about building a legacy.

Another valuable tool in community engagement is collaboration with schools and educational institutions. Police officers who visit schools, give talks, or participate in career days can plant the seed of interest in law enforcement at an early age. Programs that offer mentorships, internships, or even partnerships with high schools or colleges create pathways for students to explore policing as a career. Youth mentorship initiatives are particularly effective in guiding young people, providing them with positive role models and insight into the values and responsibilities of law enforcement. By building these connections early, agencies can create a pipeline of motivated, community-focused candidates.

Take your relationship with local colleges and universities to the next level by forging partnerships with their criminal justice, political science, and other relevant degree programs. These institutions often measure their success by the percentage of graduates who secure employment immediately after graduation. By working together, you can create a mutually beneficial pathway that connects students with opportunities in your agency while enhancing the school's employment statistics.

Start by sending guest lecturers to speak at these institutions. Perhaps you can discuss the laws surrounding search and seizure at a legal course or share your opinion on the Broken Window Theory during a criminology lecture. Colleges and professors love having outside speakers present to their classes to provide a well-rounded educational experience for their students.

Don't limit your outreach to senior classes; aim to build visibility and rapport with students throughout their college journey. Engage with underclassmen early to plant the seeds of interest in your agency and follow up with them as they progress in their academic careers. By maintaining a consistent presence, your agency can establish itself as a desirable employer and a natural career destination for these aspiring professionals.

As students near graduation, communicate clearly about the opportunities with your agency and guide them through the application process. If your background checks and hiring procedures take four to five months to complete, encourage them to apply early enough to secure a position before graduation. Collaborate with them to accommodate their class schedules during the process. Over time, this partnership can evolve into a dependable pipeline of highly qualified candidates, strengthening your agency and the university's reputation for career placement.

Citizen police academies provide another important avenue for community engagement and recruitment. These programs invite residents to participate in hands-on learning experiences that give them an insider's view of police work. Participants learn about various aspects of law enforcement, such as investigations, use of force, and the challenges officers face. This enhances public understanding of the profession and piques interest in law enforcement careers among participants. Additionally, it helps develop ambassadors within the community who can advocate for law enforcement and encourage others to consider the field.

Ride-along programs also play a crucial role in fostering positive relationships with your community. By allowing civilians to accompany officers on their shifts, these programs provide a transparent look into the daily lives of law enforcement personnel. Ride-alongs can be particularly influential for individuals considering a career in law enforcement, as they offer real-world exposure to the challenges and rewards of the profession. Participants gain a deeper appreciation for the complexities of police work, and this experience often strengthens their desire to serve their communities in a law enforcement capacity. Furthermore, candidates often feel a stronger connection with agencies that inspired and convinced them to join the profession. Highlight the ride-along opportunity for those interested in law enforcement on your agency's website and social media platforms. By providing these ride-along opportunities, you can increase your chances of attracting interested candidates to your department.

Youth engagement programs, such as Police Explorer programs or cadet initiatives, provide a more structured approach to recruiting younger generations. These programs introduce young people to the fundamentals of law enforcement and offer them opportunities to develop leadership skills, discipline, and a sense of civic duty. By immersing participants in the world of policing early on, agencies can nurture a long-term interest in law enforcement careers. These programs also serve as a platform to identify and mentor potential recruits, guiding them toward future professional success.

Ultimately, community engagement is not just about filling vacancies; it's about fostering a sense of shared responsibility and ownership over public safety. When your citizens feel they have a stake in their community's law enforcement, they are more likely to see policing as a fulfilling and honorable career path. By involving the community at every stage of the recruitment process, agencies can attract candidates who are skilled, capable, and deeply invested in the well-being of the community they will serve.

Engaging members of the community is essential to the future of law enforcement recruitment. Agencies can build trust and attract a diverse and qualified pool of candidates through proactive involvement in local events, schools, and mentorship programs. Programs like ride-along, citizen academies, and youth initiatives provide invaluable insights into the profession and help inspire the next generation of officers. By prioritizing relationships and actively working to reflect the communities they serve, law enforcement agencies can create a more robust, representative workforce better equipped to face the challenges of modern policing.

# CHAPTER EIGHT
# MOVING FORWARD

$L$aw enforcement stands at a crossroads. The challenges agencies have faced with recruiting and retaining officers in today's environment are not momentary hurdles. They are indicators of a cultural transformation. If we are to build law enforcement agencies that thrive in the years ahead, we must move beyond the outdated playbooks of the past and embrace a future that is strategic, data-driven, and adaptable.

We've explored the struggles departments face in bringing in and keeping good officers. We've talked about the importance of adapting recruitment strategies to attract a new generation, the role of technology in streamlining hiring processes, and the need to leverage social media to meet candidates where they are. We've broken down the necessity of tracking key performance indicators (KPIs) to measure what's working and what's not. And we've emphasized that building community trust isn't just a public relations effort; it's the foundation of every agency's success. Now, the question is: Where do we go from here?

## PREDICTING THE FUTURE OF LAW ENFORCEMENT RECRUITMENT AND RETENTION

Looking ahead, the future of law enforcement recruitment and retention will be shaped by shifting societal expectations, technologi-

COLIN WHITTINGTON

cal advancements, and evolving workforce priorities. Agencies that fail to recognize these changes will struggle, while those that proactively adapt will emerge stronger and more resilient.

I fear that one of the most significant trends in the coming years will be the increasing difficulty of attracting candidates to policing. Public perception of law enforcement has fluctuated dramatically in recent years. Departments must work harder than ever to show potential recruits that this profession remains an honorable and rewarding career. Younger generations, particularly Millennials and Gen Z, have different expectations than their predecessors. They value purpose-driven work, professional development, and flexibility, three factors that many police agencies have historically overlooked in their recruiting strategies. Departments that ignore these priorities will find themselves unable to compete for top talent.

Technology will also play a major role in shaping recruitment and retention. Artificial intelligence and data analytics will help streamline hiring processes, making it easier to identify and engage qualified candidates. Applicant tracking systems (ATS) will become the norm, allowing agencies to manage large pools of candidates efficiently while maintaining consistent communication. Social media and digital platforms will continue to dominate recruitment efforts, requiring agencies to invest in compelling content that resonates with tech-savvy candidates. Departments that fail to integrate these tools will be left behind.

Retention will become an even more significant challenge as law enforcement agencies compete not just with other departments but with private-sector jobs offering better work-life balance, remote work options, and competitive salaries. If policing is to remain an attractive career choice, agencies must address officer wellness, career development, and leadership training. The departments that invest in their people through mentorship programs, mental health resources, and clear promotional pathways will be the ones that maintain stability, while others struggle with constant turnover.

Community engagement will no longer be optional but a core function of every officer's role. In the past, many agencies viewed community outreach as a separate initiative, often relegated to specialized units or public relations officers. However, in the evolving landscape of law enforcement, fostering trust and collaboration with the community must be a daily responsibility shared by every member of the department. This means going beyond traditional neighborhood watch meetings and actively engaging with residents through social media, local events, and open forums. Officers must be seen not just as enforcers of the law but as problem solvers, mentors, and advocates for the communities they serve. Agencies that integrate community engagement into their training, performance evaluations, and overall culture will build stronger relationships with the people they protect.

Departments that measure and analyze their recruitment and retention efforts, factoring in public perception, community feedback, and officer satisfaction, will sustain long-term success. Utilizing Key Performance Indicators (KPIs) in all facets of recruiting and retention will become paramount in a world where the smallest details can be the difference between a well-staffed agency and one struggling to respond to the needs of its citizens. Agencies must adapt their hiring strategies to reflect the needs of the people they serve, ensuring that law enforcement remains a respected and appealing profession.

The future is not set in stone. Law enforcement leaders can adapt and evolve or remain stagnant and suffer the consequences. Agencies that refuse to modernize their recruitment efforts, embrace technology, or invest in officer wellness will face an increasing struggle to attract and retain quality personnel. Departments that fail to listen to the concerns of their officers and communities will experience higher turnover rates, lower morale, and diminished public trust.

Conversely, those who take proactive steps to refine their hiring processes, enhance professional development opportunities, and prioritize work-life balance will create environments where officers want to stay and grow. Change will not happen overnight, nor will it be easy, but the departments that take a strategic and forward-thinking approach will be the ones that thrive. The responsibility falls on law enforcement leaders at all levels to set the tone, drive innovation, and ensure that policing remains an honorable and sustainable career choice for future generations.

## A MINDSET SHIFT

For too long, law enforcement has relied on tradition as the guiding principle for recruitment and retention. But the reality is that we can no longer afford to operate under the assumption that "this is the way we've always done it" is a valid excuse for inaction. Instead, agencies must embrace a mindset of continuous improvement that prioritizes adaptability, innovation, and proactive engagement.

Leadership at all levels must recognize that recruiting is no longer just the job of a hiring unit. It is the responsibility of every officer, every supervisor, and every law enforcement executive. Retention is not just about offering competitive pay and benefits; it's about fostering a culture where officers feel valued, supported, and equipped with the tools they need to succeed. Recruitment is not just about filling vacancies; it's about shaping the future of policing with the right people for the job.

Modern recruiting strategies must evolve beyond the outdated approaches of the past. Agencies need to engage candidates through social media, targeted digital marketing, and outreach efforts designed specifically for younger generations. Traditional job fairs and outdated websites won't cut it anymore. Departments that fail to adapt their recruitment efforts to the digital landscape will struggle to connect with the very people they need to attract.

To reach a younger, more tech-savvy audience, agencies should prioritize video content, live Q&A sessions, and behind-the-scenes glimpses of what it means to serve as an officer. Many young professionals are hesitant to join law enforcement because of misconceptions about the job, negative portrayals in the media, or a lack of understanding about career advancement opportunities. Transparency and storytelling can go a long way in reshaping public perception and making the profession more appealing.

Additionally, departments must take a hard look at their hiring requirements and evaluate whether they are truly selecting the best candidates or inadvertently turning away qualified individuals due to outdated policies. Some agencies still rely on extensive, antiquated testing methods that do not accurately measure an applicant's ability to perform the job effectively. Others automatically disqualify candidates for minor infractions from years past, mistakes that have no real bearing on their potential to serve with integrity and professionalism.

Even more concerning, many departments continue to enforce strict grooming and appearance policies, such as prohibitions on visible tattoos or facial hair, that needlessly exclude highly capable and motivated candidates, particularly from younger generations. These rigid standards shrink the hiring pool and create an unnecessary barrier to attracting individuals who could bring fresh perspectives and diverse experiences to policing. While maintaining high ethical and professional standards is crucial, agencies must critically assess whether their hiring criteria are truly relevant to modern law enforcement or if they are pushing away the very people who could help shape the profession's future. Adaptability and open-mindedness in hiring practices will be essential to ensuring that law enforcement agencies remain competitive in recruiting the next generation of officers.

Technology must play a bigger role in hiring. Applicant tracking systems (ATS) can revolutionize the recruitment process by making it more efficient, transparent, and data-driven. These systems help agencies streamline applications, track candidate progress, and improve communication with potential recruits. By integrating technology into hiring practices, agencies can reduce delays, increase efficiency, and ensure they're not losing qualified applicants due to outdated processes and unnecessarily lengthy background processes.

Beyond recruitment, agencies must harness technology to enhance officer satisfaction and performance. Many departments still struggle with outdated scheduling systems, ineffective training methods, and burdensome paperwork, which hinder efficiency and morale. By adopting modern digital solutions such as mobile scheduling apps, virtual training platforms, and AI-driven crime analysis, agencies can streamline operations, reduce administrative strain, and empower officers to focus on their core responsibilities. Moreover, these technological advancements serve as powerful recruitment tools, attracting tech-savvy candidates eager to leverage innovation in their law enforcement careers.

Data analytics must become a cornerstone of law enforcement recruitment and retention strategies. Agencies should not rely on guesswork or outdated methods to assess their hiring and retention success; instead, they must leverage measurable data to drive decision-making. Key performance indicators such as application-to-hire conversion rates, retention rates by tenure, and engagement levels in professional development programs provide valuable insights into what's working and what needs improvement. By tracking these metrics over time, agencies can identify trends, pinpoint problem areas, and adjust their strategies accordingly. For example, if data reveals a high dropout rate during the hiring process, agencies can analyze where candidates are disengaging and make necessary changes to improve applicant experiences. If retention rates are declining among mid-career officers, leadership can investigate factors such as job satisfaction, career advancement opportunities, and workload distribution. Furthermore, analyzing engagement in training and mentorship programs can help departments understand whether their investments in professional development are truly benefiting officers or if adjustments need to be made. By embracing a data-driven approach, agencies can make informed decisions about where to allocate resources, optimize recruitment efforts, and create a workplace culture that supports long-term officer retention.

COLIN WHITTINGTON

One of the most significant shifts agencies must make is recognizing that recruitment and retention are not just HR functions. They are fundamental organizational priorities that impact every aspect of policing. Too often, these responsibilities are viewed as the sole domain of human resources or recruitment officers when, in reality, they require a department-wide commitment. Every officer, from the newest recruit to the most seasoned veteran, plays a role in shaping the department's future. How officers talk about their agency, how they mentor new hires, and how leadership fosters a sense of purpose all contribute to whether an agency is seen as an attractive place to build a career. Retaining great officers isn't just about offering competitive salaries; it's about creating an environment where people feel valued, supported, and motivated to stay. A strong departmental culture, one that prioritizes professional development, recognizes achievements, and encourages collaboration, can be the deciding factor in whether an officer stays for decades or walks away after a few years.

Mentorship programs should be a cornerstone of an officer's career, offering structured guidance and support that fosters long-term commitment to the profession. Too often, young officers are thrown into the field without a clear roadmap for career growth or an understanding of how to navigate the challenges of the job. A well-designed mentorship program pairs new recruits with experienced officers who can provide insight, encouragement, and real-world advice, helping them build confidence and resilience.

Additionally, leadership development must extend far beyond promotional exams. Officers should be trained in the skills necessary to lead, inspire, and retain their peers, not just to enforce policies but to cultivate a positive work environment. Leadership should not be reserved for those with rank; agencies must instill leadership qualities in every officer, empowering them to contribute to the department's mission and culture.

Furthermore, officer wellness must be a top priority, not just a box to check. Mental health support, peer assistance programs, and work-life balance initiatives should be fully integrated into agency operations, ensuring officers can access real, practical solutions that improve job satisfaction and overall well-being. When officers feel professionally and personally supported, they are more likely to stay committed to their careers, communities, and departments for the long haul.

## MY CHALLENGE TO YOU

Moving forward, law enforcement agencies must take full ownership of their future. Recruitment and retention challenges cannot be solved by maintaining the status quo. The path ahead requires intentionality, strong leadership, and a willingness to evolve. Policing is at a crossroads, and the decisions made today will determine whether agencies thrive or continue to struggle in the years to come. Those who cling to outdated methods, rigid policies, and resistance to change will find themselves left behind, unable to attract or retain the talent necessary to fulfill their mission. However, those who embrace innovation, data-driven strategies, and a commitment to officer wellness will strengthen their ranks, rebuild public trust, and foster a new generation of dedicated officers.

For police executives, this means committing to long-term change rather than settling for short-term fixes. It requires looking beyond immediate hiring needs and investing in sustainable solutions that create a workplace where officers feel valued and supported. Leaders must proactively identify emerging challenges, adopt policies, and ensure their agencies remain competitive in attracting top-tier candidates. For officers, it means taking personal responsibility for shaping the future of the profession by mentoring new recruits, promoting a culture of excellence, and embracing new ways of policing that strengthen community relationships. The profession will only be as strong as the men and women who uphold its values every day. And for communities, it means recognizing that supporting law enforcement goes beyond simply backing the badge. It's about advocating for well-trained, well-equipped, and well-supported officers who can serve with integrity, professionalism, and empathy.

COLIN WHITTINGTON

Public safety is a shared responsibility. When law enforcement and communities work together as true partners, listening to each other, addressing concerns, and striving for meaningful progress, both become stronger, safer, and more resilient.

The future of law enforcement is being written right now. Every policy change, every recruitment decision, and every leadership choice is shaping what comes next. The question is: Will we seize this opportunity to build something better?

The answer must be yes.

And it starts today.

# ABOUT THE AUTHOR

Colin Whittington is a former deputy sheriff and the Founder and Chief Executive Officer of Recruiting Heroes LLC. Colin started his law enforcement career as a patrol deputy for the Loudoun County Sheriff's Office, the largest, full-service sheriff's office in Virginia. Within his first two years, he received two Life Saving Awards for two separate incidents. In 2019, Colin was named the Virginia Deputy Sheriff of the Year by the Virginia Sheriff's Association. Colin was then promoted to Sergeant and was charged with running the recruiting, background investigation, and hiring unit for the Loudoun County Sheriff's Office. He supervised a team of recruiters and

COLIN WHITTINGTON

background investigators. While law enforcement agencies around the nation struggled to attract talent, Colin's team led the agency to a record-low vacancy rate through innovative and strategic recruiting strategies.

Colin left law enforcement in 2022 and became the recruiting director for an information technology firm in northern Virginia, where he recruited top talent for positions with the federal government and major corporations. During this time, Colin never forgot his brothers and sisters on the Thin Blue Line. He received countless messages from police officers, deputy sheriffs, and federal agents from around America seeking advice and help on how they could successfully transition to the private sector.

The lack of resources available to our law enforcement officers inspired Colin to start his own business. Recruiting Heroes LLC is an employment agency dedicated to finding amazing careers for America's veterans and first responders. Colin and his team work with companies and candidates around the country. He offers resume writing, LinkedIn profile optimization, and interview training for officers looking to find new careers after their years of service. Recruiting Heroes helps companies looking to bring fantastic candidates to their teams, particularly those looking to hire veterans and first responders. Colin is also proud to offer recruiting and retention services for law enforcement agencies around America.

Colin became a best-selling author in July 2024 with his debut book, Beyond the Thin Blue Line. The book has sold thousands of copies around the world and continues to play a vital part in the career transition of law enforcement officers everywhere.

In his free time, Colin enjoys spending time with his family, playing soccer, and competing in Ironman triathlons.

www.WhittingtonBooks.com

Colin.Whittington@RecruitingHeroesLLC.com

www.ingramcontent.com/pod-product-compliance
Lightning Source LLC
Chambersburg PA
CBHW061800120626
46550CB00005B/2073